Susan L. Mitchell

THE IRISH WRITERS SERIES
James F. Carens, General Editor

TITLE	*AUTHOR*
SEAN O'CASEY	Bernard Benstock
J. C. MANGAN	James Kilroy
W. R. RODGERS	Darcy O'Brien
STANDISH O'GRADY	Phillip L. Marcus
PAUL VINCENT CARROLL	Paul A. Doyle
SEUMAS O'KELLY	George Brandon Saul
SHERIDAN LEFANU	Michael Begnal
AUSTIN CLARKE	John Jordan
BRIAN FRIEL	D. E. S. Maxwell
DANIEL CORKERY	George Brandon Saul
EIMAR O'DUFFY	Robert Hogan
MERVYN WALL	Robert Hogan
FRANK O'CONNOR	James Matthews
GEORGE MOORE	Janet Egleson
JAMES JOYCE	Fritz Senn
JOHN BUTLER YEATS	Douglas Archibald
LORD EDWARD DUNSANY	Zack Bowen
MARIA EDGEWORTH	James Newcomer
MARY LAVIN	Zack Bowen
OSCAR WILDE	Edward Partridge
SOMERVILLE AND ROSS	John Cronin
SUSAN L. MITCHELL	Richard M. Kain
J. M. SYNGE	Robin Skelton
KATHARINE TYNAN	Marilyn Gaddis Rose
LIAM O'FLAHERTY	James O'Brien
IRIS MURDOCH	Donna Gerstenberger
JAMES STEPHENS	Birgit Bramsback
BENEDICT KIELY	Daniel Casey
EDWARD MARTYN	Robert Christopher
BRENDAN BEHAN	John Stewart Collis
DOUGLAS HYDE	Gareth Dunleavy
EDNA O'BRIEN	Grace Eckley
CHARLES LEVER	M. S. Elliott
BRIAN MOORE	Jeanne Flood
SAMUEL BECKETT	Clive Hart
ELIZABETH BOWEN	Edwin J. Kenney
JOHN MONTAGUE	Frank Kersnowski
ROBERT MATURIN	Robert E. Lougy
GEORGE FITZMAURICE	Arthur E. McGuinness
MICHAEL MCCLAVERTY	Leo F. McNamara
FRANCIS STUART	J. H. Natterstad
PATRICK KAVANAGH	Darcy O'Brien
BRINSLEY MACNAMARA	Raymond J. Porter
AND GEORGE SHIELS	
STEPHEN MACKENNA	Roger Rosenblatt
JACK B. YEATS	Robin Skelton
WILLIAM ALLINGHAM	Alan Warner
SAMUEL LOVER	Mabel Worthington
FLANN O'BRIEN	Bernard Benstock
DENIS JOHNSTON	James F. Carens
WILLIAM LARMINIE	Richard J. Finneran

SUSAN L. MITCHELL

Richard M. Kain

LEWISBURG
BUCKNELL UNIVERSITY PRESS

© 1972 by Associated University Presses, Inc.

Associated University Presses, Inc.
Cranbury, New Jersey 08512

Library of Congress Cataloging in Publication Data

Kain, Richard Morgan, 1908–
    Susan L. Mitchell.

    (The Irish writers series)
    Bibliography: p.
    1. Mitchell, Susan L. I. Title.
PR6025.I847Z7   821′.9′12   78-126275
ISBN 0-8387-7768-6
ISBN 0-8387-7627-2 (pbk.)

Contents

Acknowledgments   7

Chronology   9

1. "The Personal Ever Delighted Me"—
   Susan Mitchell in Her Time   13

2. *Aids to the Immortality of Certain Persons
   in Ireland*   35

3. *The Living Chalice*   64

4. *George Moore (1916)*   77

5. The Laughter that Opens the Heart   90

Selected Bibliography   97

Acknowledgments

Each of my Irish friends and every Irish scholar has contributed to my knowledge of the tradition of Ireland and the spirit of Anglo-Irish literature. I must limit my acknowledgments to those specifically connected with this manuscript.

In Dublin: the late Mr. Constantine Curran; Mr. M. Byrne, Public Record Office; Miss Frances-Jane French; the late Eoin O'Mahony. In Sligo, Miss Nora Niland, County Sligo Museum; in Armagh, Mr. D. R. M. Weatherup, County Armagh Museum. Also, Mr. Charles H. Gibbs-Smith, Victoria and Albert Museum, London; Dr. Malcolm Brown, University of Washington, Seattle; Dr. Janet Egleson Dunleavy, University of Wisconsin at Milwaukee and her daughter, Miss Karen Egleson; Mr. Tom Ware, University of Tennessee at Chattanooga; and Dr. James O'Brien, Western Washington State College. Finally, and most gratefully, Miss Mitchell's niece, Mrs. Dora McGuinness, of Toronto; Mrs. Josef Solterer, daughter of Constantine Curran, Washington, D.C.; Mr. Patrick Henchy, National

Library of Ireland, Dublin; and Mr. Alan Denson, bibliographer and editor of A.E., Kendal, Westmorland, England. The many kindnesses and instances of generosity represented by these names deserve much more than I can here state.

Numerous inquiries have failed to discover any copyright owner of Susan Mitchell's work. The quotations in this volume are used solely to evoke the quality of her writing and the charm of her personality. In no sense do they represent her fully, nor do they constitute an anthology. Should any heir be identified, appropriate permission fees can be arranged.

The portrait of Susan Mitchell is reproduced by the kind permission of Mrs. Solterer, who inherited it from her mother, Mrs. Constantine Curran, the "Honor Lavelle" of the Abbey Theatre and the Theatre of Ireland. It is a drawing by J. B. Yeats the elder, probably 1902 or 1903, certainly between 1902 and 1908.

Chronology

1866   Susan Langstaff Mitchell born at Carrick-on-Shannon.

1872   Death of her father led to separation of family. Susan moved to Dublin, where she was raised by her aunts, who later went with Susan to Birr, hometown of the Mitchell family, where her uncle was Crown Solicitor, an office held by a Mitchell for three generations. After the death of the aunts, Susan stayed briefly in Sligo, helping two younger sisters with a school they had recently taken over.

1899–
1900   Undergoing treatment in London, she lived with the family of J. B. Yeats.

1901   Sub-editor of *The Irish Homestead,* edited by H. F. Norman; then, about 1905, by AE. Lived with her mother and sister until her mother's death, then with her sister and nieces.

1902–
1908   Poems in holiday supplement of *The Irish Home-*

stead, *A Celtic Christmas*. See Bibliography for
this and other publications.

1904   Five poems included in *New Songs*.

1907   Poem in *The Abbey Row*.

1908   *Aids to the Immortality of Certain Persons in Ireland, Charitably Administered*.

1908   *The Living Chalice and Other Poems*.

1911   Dramatic skit in *The Irish Review*, "Leaguers and Peelers; or, the Apple Cart."

1912   Cuala Press collection of verse, *Frankincense and Myrrh*.

1913   Second, enlarged editions of volumes published in 1908.

1916   *George Moore*, "Irishmen of To-Day" series.

1918   "Preface" to *Secret Springs of Dublin Song*.

1923–

1926   Sub-editor of *The Irish Statesman*, second series.

1926   Death, after lingering illness.

Susan L. Mitchell

1

"The Personal Ever Delighted Me"—Susan Mitchell in Her Time

As an amused observer and minor participant in the Irish Literary Revival, Susan Mitchell earned her place in the story, though her genial talent has been obscured by the brighter luminaries of her generation. Her work was scarcely mentioned in Ernest Boyd's early but still basic account, *Ireland's Literary Renaissance* (1916; rev. 1922), and in recent years she has been accorded only an extensive note by Alan Denson in his edition of AE's letters (1961) and a short but perceptive essay by Robin Skelton in *The World of Yeats* (1965). Her witty verses on the events of her day bring the Dublin scene before our eyes. With playful humor she records those controversies and clashes of personality which appear in the recollections of George Moore and William Butler Yeats—disputes over the Municipal Gallery and the riots during the opening week of Synge's "The Playboy of the Western World," as well as arguments about the revival of the Irish language, and the intransigence of Ulster. Her lilting meters contain rapier thrusts at bombast and pretence. Her mockery is, for the most part, free of malice. The delightful title of her book of satires, *Aids to the Immortality of Certain Persons in Ireland*, has as its conclusion *Charitably Administered*. In regard to her charity, George Moore was a notable exception. Her amusing foreword to *Aids* anticipates the objection, "There is too much George Moore in it," then refutes or deflects the complaint with the artful dodge of suggesting a worse alternative: "be thankful that when I chose a George to write about it was not George Bernard Shaw; that I gave you some one you can understand and be superior about, and did not ask you to seat yourselves on a volcano and play with forked lightning." An irrefutable way this, of minimizing the satire by depreciating the importance of its victim. The first poem in *Aids,* entitled "George Moore Comes to Ireland," uncovers the pomposity of the literary prodigal who returned to discover his native land, to shock it while taking a leading hand in its cultural revival, and to turn away from it in disdain:

My naughty, problematic past was nothing but a sham,
My sins and my repentance all paper and all cram.
Some day you'll all discover how respectable I am,
How I revere the marriage state, believe in Abraham,
And for Gaels and their revivals don't really care a damn!

We shall hear more of George later.

There were several other Susan Mitchells. In addition to her light verse—almost unique in this period—she was the author of competent poetry in the mood of the Celtic Twilight, modest, meditative, traditional, not unlike the dreamed-of work by James Joyce's Walter Mitty, Little Chandler of "A Little Cloud." With subtle irony Joyce described how Chandler passes "the poor stunted houses" as he walks from his clerk's desk to an appointment with his erstwhile friend, now a successful journalist back from London on a visit:

> Melancholy was the dominant note of his temperament, he thought, but it was a melancholy tempered by recurrences of faith and resignation and simple joy. If he could give expression to it in a book of poems perhaps men would listen.

Discounting any possibility of popularity, he imagines the phrases with which his poems would be greeted by the English crtics:

> *"Mr. Chandler has the gift of easy and graceful verse."* ... *"A wistful sadness pervades these poems."* ... *"The Celtic note."*

How many struck "the Celtic note" in those days! Especially the women—Ellen O'Leary, Rose Kavanagh, Eva Gore-Booth, Rosa Mulholland, and Ella Young come to mind. The 500-page bibliography of D. J. O'Donoghue's *The Poets of Ireland* (1912) contains hundreds of now-forgotten names. In Susan Mitchell's case, a number of her religious poems deserve to be rescued from oblivion. Often confessional in tone, they convey intimacy with one temperamentally inclined towards a vocation. The title is significant. The poet regards herself as *The Living Chalice,* ready, albeit reluctantly, for the Lord's service.

Another phase of her career was manifested in her devoted editorial assistance to AE (George William Russell) in his work on *The Irish Homestead* and *The Irish Statesman.* There were strong personal ties between Susan Mitchell and the gentle mystic of so many talents. Russell's obituary tribute to her in the March 13, 1926 issue of *The Irish Statesman* expresses his sorrow at the loss of "the kindest and most reliable of friends," whose work was informed by "a delightful wit, sentences shaped with a rare grace, and a humanity so kindly and tolerant and understanding that it seemed the consummation of womanly wisdom." She was "one of the best Irish women of her time, capable of following the profoundest thinking and of illuminating it by some flash of her own intuition." Russell concluded with a moving statement, expressing hesitantly the hope that she be not forgotten:

> The memory of that gay, wise, ever kind and unselfish spirit will last while they have life with all who knew her. The image which that woman of genius made in the souls of her friends will stand up for long even against the assailings of Time.

It has often been said that Russell never overcame his bereavement.

Russell gave voice to his desolation at her death in a letter to Ernest Boyd, apologizing for a delay in printing a review of Boyd's *Studies in Ten Literatures.* "It was not forgetfulness which caused no review to appear," he wrote, "but the long illness of Susan Mitchell during which I was doing double duty with a very heavy heart." Of her death he wrote:

> a great blow to me, indeed the heaviest I ever felt in my life because she was the kindest and most unselfish of colleagues for over twenty years. I never lost any friend with whom I had been in daily association and it leaves a terrible gap in my life. I suppose time will cover this up by degrees but since last Christmas up to the present I am more oppressed in my mind and heart than I ever had been and I have to drive my pen to get an article written. In old days my thought ran before the pen.
>
> (*Letters from AE,* edited by Alan Denson (1961), p. 170)

AE published a retrospective review of Susan Mitchell's poetry which opened with the observation that "It is but a little part of life can be reflected in literature." In literature and in memory alike. There remain but a few scattered recollections, such as those of Beatrice Elvery, later Lady Glenavy. When Miss Elvery was about to leave the stained-glass workshop of Sarah Purser for the Slade School in London, Susan Mitchell wrote a song for the farewell dinner. As Lady Glenavy recalls, "The Dublin United Arts Club welcomed any excuse for a club dinner and my departure seemed to provide an excellent one." The song was unexpectedly gentle:

> It might not seem the most enviable experience to be hymned by such a sharp tongue, but Susan Mitchell re-

lented in my case. Her little song about me was to the
tune of 'She's over the border and awa' ', and it ran:

> Our pretty Beatrice departs
> To win her Art more grace,
> But she'll not fashion anything
> More lovely than her face.
> Apollo asks a sacrifice,
> With grief our hearts o'erflow.
> Oh, must we offer at his shrine
> The loveliest thing we know?
> ('*Today We Will Only Gossip*' (1964), p. 49)

The present writer knows of two portraits, reflective
perhaps of the two sides of Susan Mitchell's nature, the
serious and the playful. A surprisingly formal oil by
J. B. Yeats, the poet's father, now in the National Gallery
of Ireland and reproduced by Alan Denson in his exhaustive bibliography, *Printed Writings by George W.
Russell (A E)* (1961), reveals a steady gaze on a classical
face, unsmiling. The hair is softly parted in the middle.
The subject is wearing a somewhat formal Edwardian
wide-necked dress with white ruffled collar. In a slightly
contrasting mood, a pencil sketch, also by J. B. Yeats,
has a carefree informality, catching the subject with a
momentary tilt of the head, as though she were just
turning to listen to a chance remark. The same steady,
unsmiling gaze is there, but the casualness of the pose
captures that warmth of personality and air of intimacy
so often achieved by the elder Yeats in his drawings.

When AE closed his Dublin house he gave this sketch
to his close friend and neighbor, Mrs. Constantine
Curran, who, under the stage name of Honor Lavelle,

had been the first to play the role of Maurya in Synge's *Riders to the Sea*. Her daughter Elizabeth (Mrs. Josef Solterer) has sent me a photograph and has been equally generous with her recollections of a dear family friend:

> At parties here & in her own house I can remember her always reciting something new—of the moment—in the same vein—always fresh, sharp but not cruel. She was one of the gayest, most feminine and amusing personalities I can remember. . . .

The friendship was of long standing: "Susan was first my mother's intimate in the early days of the National Theatre Soc. and the Hermetic Society with AE at which time she was working in some secretarial capacity in the Co-operative Movement. . . . She worked as you know side by side with AE in the Homestead & Irish Statesman editorial office until her death. All my schooldays she lived with her sister a block from AE on Rathgar Avenue & 5 mins from here."

In a charming letter, J. B. Yeats compared her to a kitten of his, "so playful and tender, such big eyes, such soft paws, and such claws, only it *is a boy* I would have it christened Susan." (J. B. Yeats, *Letters. . . .* ed. Joseph Hone (1944), p. 60) The painter's letter to her, evaluating her poetry, contains some mild criticism:

> Every now and then I turn to your few poems and like them better and better—it is because you have such a poignant way of dropping suddenly into some personal 'particular.' It is what I call your naïveté—and because of it you have something which I find neither in AE or in W. B. Y. I think it might be called a *quality of intensity*. If you would write more and *use your own life*

more, we should have not only more poetry, but it would be stronger and more intimate. (*Ibid.,* p. 150)

An afterthought qualifies this advice a day later in keeping with the painter-philosopher's concern with the impersonality of art: "I ought to have said that the intensity by the time it reaches its expression is no longer *personal,* entering into the world of art, the personal ego is dropped away—for I think personal art is bad art, at any rate second rate." (*Ibid.,* p. 152) A week later he reiterates to his son that "She is poet through and through and with intensity—a beautiful intensity that only half unveils itself—she has naïveté and is full of *'particulars'* and she has the impersonality of true personality—she gives herself to what she touches." (*Ibid.,* p. 154)

All evidence points to her charm and vivacity. Thus Seumas O'Sullivan in his essay:

one of the most fascinating women I have ever met. Still lovely to look upon, though no longer in the dazzling splendour and colour which glow for us in that fine early portrait by Sarah Purser; lovely, too, to listen to with her deep musical voice, her glorious and irresistible laugh which lit up the stream of her witty talk, like sunlight on a river. She was one of the few wits I have known, whose wit and satire held nothing malicious. She was, too, one of the most unopinionated of people, and for all her appearance of assurance, one of the shyest.

(*Essays and Recollections* (1944), p. 123)

Biographical information is meagre, but a memoir by her niece, Bidz Dora Brabazon McGuinness, contains

considerable information and corroborates what has
been said of her personality. She was born in 1866, at
Carrick-on-Shannon, a town evoked in one of her poems.
Her father, manager of the Provincial Bank, died in
1872, leaving his family of seven children in straitened
circumstances. The mother moved to Sligo and raised
the four younger children. The two eldest were taken
by a maternal aunt in Sligo, and Susan was sent to
Dublin at the age of six, in the care of two of her father's
sisters. To quote the memoir:

> These aunts were comfortably off and Susan lacked for
> nothing. She attended daily a good private school for girls
> on Morehampton Road and in addition had the best tui-
> tion available for music, singing and drawing and dancing
> lessons.

Shortly before she joined AE as assistant editor of *The
Irish Homestead* in 1901, she was stricken with an illness which required treatment in London, where she
stayed with the Yeats family. It is regrettable that she
never wrote the book she planned about this fascinating
family and her stay with them.

The memoir throws a poignant light upon one of
Miss Mitchell's beautiful poems, "The Music of the
Silence." Without knowledge of the circumstances, it
can be read as a wistful evocation of the loneliness of
the human condition:

> I cannot hear the trembling speech of grass,
> Nor the shy little voices of the wind,
> I cannot hear the happy talk doth pass
> Between my friends, nor in it meaning find.

In actual fact, illness had impaired her hearing, and these lines are literally true. Mrs. McGuinness observes that "To one with her love of music and the sound of words, the shock of her deafness must have come with shattering impact."

Another recollection is that of John Eglinton, in *A Memoir of AE* (1937). Eglinton remarks that despite her poor health she "always maintained a sly cheerfulness, and became the hostess of the office." She and Russell "were a familiar sight in the streets of Dublin, catching the sardonic eye of Stephen Dedalus as he passed in his now world-famed odyssey," ie. *Ulysses*. (pp. 73–74). Eglinton's memory betrays him here. It was Bloom who encountered the two, and the identification of the woman as Susan Mitchell is not at all clear. On his way to lunch Bloom is overtaken by a "high figure in homespun, beard and bicycle, a listening woman at his side." He finds the woman careless in dress, with loose stockings, and thinks it might be Lizzie Twigg. To return to the memoir, John Eglinton says of the intimacy that it may have affected Russell's marital life, despite his puremindedness. Eglinton attributes the estrangement between George Moore and AE to Susan Mitchell's book. It has also been suggested in my hearing that Miss Mitchell's antagonism to Moore may derive from some insinuation of scandal made by the garrulous gossip of Ely Place. In that case, Miss Mitchell was able to retort in kind. Her witticism is quoted in *Ulysses* (Joyce's only indisputable reference to her): "That Moore is Martyn's wild oats."

Mrs. McGuinness describes her social evenings, where

despite the absence of liquor, "the parties were crowded" with notables, and entertainment was provided by "Talk, music, and impromptu charades":

> Susan was a kind and excellent hostess and saw to it that not only the bright and brilliant enjoyed themselves, but that the quiet and shy ones also had a happy time.

Such soirées characterize a bygone age of innocent fun, quaint and Victorian to modern readers.

In her editorial role Miss Mitchell was called upon for a steady stream of miscellaneous articles, "fillers" demanded by the size of the paper and the lack of paid contributors. It was said that AE had to adopt all sorts of pseudonyms in order to conceal the fact that he often had to write almost entire issues. The early work has not been catalogued, but Edward Doyle Smith's Ph.D. thesis, "A Survey and Index of the *Irish Statesman,* 1923–1930," completed at the University of Washington in 1966, lists nearly two hundred Susan Mitchell items in the two and a half years before her death. Book reviews appeared almost every week. "Drama Notes" was a running chronicle of the theatre, once a month or so, and numerous other essays rounded out the list.

Her casual, allusive, offhandedly personal approach can be illustrated by one of her longer essays, appropriately enough on "The 'I' in Literature." In her "puzzlement" at this modern intrusion she recalls James Russell Lowell's remarks on Thoreau, to the effect that the time comes in literature when "a struggle for fresh air" is necessary. The "I" had long before appeared in autobiography, of course, but when it entered other forms it was so perfectly disguised "that his own literary parents did not recognise him." Then comes the disarming confession:

> I often sighed for this aloofness, but could never attain it, for the personal ever delighted me.

Nowadays, "How far-off and unnecessary seem these yearnings," when even George Moore—again!—"has returned from his mild roamings . . . to sit fast at his own hearth beside the one partner perennially dear to his literary uxuriousness—himself."

The closed window was good enough for such as Charlotte Yonge in Victorian days, that "period of nightcaps and bed-curtains," but today we have Joyce, "with bigger lung power," who makes us shudder as the windows crash (the same figure was used by Virginia Woolf eight months later, when she found in Joyce the "calculated indecency of a desperate man who feels that in order to breathe he must break the windows") ("Mr. Bennett and Mrs. Brown," May 18, 1924, in *Collected Essays* (1966), I, 334).

Modern artists are like children "let into some Montessorian school, where there are no 'don'ts' for scholars, but freakishness, exuberance, and even unruliness of conduct may be taken as manifestations of genius." In such circumstances real artists, knowing their goals, enjoy themselves, "but the sham artist enjoys himself just as much." In music this is a disaster, for "how unhappy the always unmusical public," and how unhappy the singer, no longer creator of beautiful sounds but "a mere stenographer to the composers." "What Joyce in music will arise," she asks, "to deliver the singer . . . from his house of bondage?"

Recent Irish writing has revealed a host of personalities:

> juvenile finality of judgment from Ervine, exquisite literary gossip from Yeats, goodnatured appreciation from Katherine Tynan, brilliant ill-nature from Joyce.

"What a treasure chest for the literary magpies of the future to thieve and rummage in!" she exclaims, an embarrassing remark to current Joyceans, Yeatsians, *et al.* For, she concludes, "if we cannot enter into the royal minds of our writers," it is at least possible to "reach up to the small intimate things, finding our point of contact with greatness in the colour of a necktie, the fall of a lock of hair, the ribbon of an eye-glass." (October 6, 1923)

The femininity of Virginia Woolf, a dash of Irish malice, her own good-natured mockery—it is only by such a list of ingredients that once can suggest the flavor of this writing. And the mockery is as much directed at the Irish, and at the author herself, as it is to the modern artist, for after all at least half of her own poetry had approached the current notables by "the fall of a lock of hair" (this, certainly, is Yeats) or "the ribbon of an eye-glass" (probably Moore, but possibly Yeats or AE).

In her reviews one can find numerous flashes of witty insight. Of Brinsley Macnamara's play, *A Glorious Uncertainty,* she remarks that "We are slowly becoming

self-conscious here in Ireland and our writers and
dramatists are helping us to a depressing if salutary self-
realisation." As for the cast, the Abbey actors "are so
clever that if they are not given a good play they make
one." (December 8, 1923) Shakespeare is popular in
Dublin because Irish speech is closer to that of the
dramatist than the current English *"sol fa* in dialogue"
which consists of "a coinage of two or three vowel
sounds." Irish audiences seemed "actually hungry for
splendour in language," sensing the meaning of obsolete
phrases, "for they are not really parted yet from any of
them." (March 15, 1924)

Her account of the performance of Yeats's *At the
Hawk's Well* in the poet's drawingroom in the spring of
1924 recreates the scene and evokes the effect:

> The stage was in the middle of the company, yet it seemed
> remote, the beautiful verse was recited close to our ears,
> but it came to them as a far away chant, and yet with this
> studied suggestion of remoteness I have never felt any-
> thing more intimate and vivid. . . . The poignant music of
> the flute echoing the verse in the hearer's soul, the thin
> tapping to whose rhythm the players entered, the angular
> gliding movements of the players, the necromantic dance
> of the hawk, I am powerless to express the emotions they
> raised . . . . (April 12, 1924)

Describing Liam O'Flaherty's relentless realism in
the stories of *Spring Sowing,* she has a retrospective gibe
at the rioters during the week when Synge's *Playboy*
opened at the Abbey in 1907, seventeen years before.
As she recalls those "ferocious defenders of our gentle
characters" she muses that "Nowadays one could imag-

ine the police being called in to some production by an Irish writer who assumed that we were an island of saints, to protect players who insulted our intelligence and tried to filch from us our reputation for unbridled ferocity." Yet in O'Flaherty "This passion is both his power and his danger," for no one else gives the same "peculiar impression of primitive power." (October 25, 1924) With *The Informer* a year later Susan Mitchell compared O'Flaherty unfavorably with Sean O'Casey. Their dramatis personae are similar,

> but O'Casey has breathed into them a humour that brings them a shade nearer humanity. . . . O'Casey's characters dwindle into futility; they cannot act; human consciousness has entered into them just so far as to make them hesitant. O'Flaherty's characters act, and with violence, having little human consciousness, but an animal force and cunning. (October 10, 1925)

In her account of a Dublin performance of Shaw's *St. Joan,* she came to the heart of the matter. Her mockery is undisguised as she notes that the author's inveterate explanations amount to "a complete inventory of his own intellectual property down to the least egg-spoon," but the marvel is that "Mr. Shaw's plays are alive." This one would hardly expect when character is replaced by "intricate and prolonged intellectual debate." As for the theme, Shaw, "with a high-spirited-ness unabated," has managed "to snatch Joan out of the very teeth of Catholic canonisation and dump her unasked into a Protestant hagiography." The result will not please partisans of either persuasion, nor will it offend, "for he makes their case more cogently than they can, and always with an integrity of mind that earns respect." Shaw is not to be let off easily, however; regarding his faith in reason she slyly remarks that he "has his infallibilities" just like the rest of us. Yet the play "walks away, as a play should, from all heady debating," and the heroine emerges "triumphantly the Saint." (July 11, 1925)

Has anyone better described the studied effect of Yeats's prose than she did in her note on *The Bounty of Sweden*? Its "elaborate pattern" combines "simplicity and formalism," producing a complex result:

> A prose that always inveigles the reader, and can excite him to furious argument or furious agreement when sometimes a sudden passion, or even a prejudice, breaks its cadence, as a native brogue might suddenly thrust itself through an accent cultivated and formal. (August 1, 1925)

To sample these late essays, a mere portion of her extensive journalistic work, is to savor the quality of a spirit ever alert and incisive, yet sensitive to poetic and spiritual values. The area of Irish periodical literature during the Revival, with its political and literary crosscurrents, remains an almost completely untouched field, awaiting a diligent chronicler.

Susan Mitchell's first appearance in a book occurred in AE's selection of *New Songs* (1904). The volume is mentioned in the library chapter of Joyce's *Ulysses*:

> —They say we are to have a literary surprise, the quaker librarian said, friendly and earnest. Mr. Russell, rumour has it, is gathering together a sheaf of our younger poets' verses. We are all looking forward anxiously.

Joyce here commits a slight anachronism, since *New Songs* had already been published in early March, three and a half months before the June 16 commemorated in *Ulysses*. Inasmuch as Joyce had been living in Dublin for more than a year (he had returned from Paris in the preceding spring) he would certainly have been aware of the inaccuracy. Oversight it may have been, or possibly an unconscious slip occasioned by the fact that his own poems were not included.

The local success of the volume was assured. AE, the poet, painter, editor, and organizer of rural cooperatives, had become virtual spokesman of the Dublin literary scene. W. B. Yeats, already more highly regarded as a poet, was residing in London for the most part, and limiting his Irish activities to the emerging theatre. He mocked AE's amateur enthusiasm for the slightest of talent, whether his own or that of his associates. Yeats termed AE's proteges his "canary birds," a remark which made many enemies and even brought forth a reproach from his father, who, though a painter of more promise than accomplishment, had his feet on the ground in respect to the necessity for popular support. In a letter quoted by Joseph Hone in his biography of Yeats, old J. B. write:

> What I think is wrong about your way of getting a movement to work is that all movements need volunteer aid. You cannot afford to pay everyone, and when you talk about "singing canaries" and "poultry farms" it all comes back to the people for whom it was intended, and with very vivid exaggerations. (p. 221)

Almost immediately after the publication of the anthology, Yeats felt obliged to apologize for some such remark, this time attributed to Lady Gregory, though of course it may have originated with Yeats. The apology appears in that often quoted letter to AE which concludes, "Let us have no emotions, however abstract, in which there is not an athletic joy." (*Letters,* ed. Wade (1955), pp. 433–435). This pronouncement has been taken as a mark of Yeats's liberation from the "celtic twilight," and certainly the twilight mood does not appeal to current taste.

Yeats was gracious enough to assume personal identification with the mood he was now rejecting:

> Some of the poems I will probably underrate . . . because the dominant mood in many of them is one I have fought in myself and put down. In my *Land of Heart's Desire,* and in some of my lyric verse of that time, there is an exaggeration of sentiment and sentimental beauty which I have come to think unmanly. . . . As so often happens with a thing one has been tempted by and is still a little tempted by, I am roused by it to a kind of frenzied hatred which is quite out of my control. (*Ibid.*)

He did commend two poems: "Miss Gore-Booth's little poem about the roads is charming and delights my conscience" (this is the anthology favorite, "The Waves of Breffny",) and, he continues, "I like the poem about the wise dead under grass and the strong gone over sea, but it leaves my conscience hungry." Yeats here refers to Seumas O'Sullivan's poem, "The Twilight People," whose whispering voices are to be heard amid the hills. The second stanza is the one Yeats had in mind:

Twilight people why will you still be crying,

Crying and calling to me out of the trees?
For under the quiet grass the wise are lying
And all the strong ones are gone over the seas.

According to Joyce, in the same discussion in *Ulysses,*
Yeats also commended the phrase "As in wild earth a
Grecian vase." It is the concluding line of the first poem,
Padraic Colum's "A Portrait," which depicts a hedge-
scholar of the forties, imparting to his charges not pa-
triotic ideals but the riches of Latin and Greek:

> But what avail my teaching slight?
> Years hence in rustic speech, a phrase,
> As in wild earth a Grecian vase.

AE's brief prefatory note to *New Songs* testifies not
only to his proverbial generosity to new talents, but to
his agreement with Yeats that Irish poetry must reject
the conventional patriotism of the nineteenth century,
associated with *The Nation,* founded in 1842 and sup-
pressed in 1848. With the exception of Miss Alice Milligan, whose patriotic poetry was to be published sep-
arately, "There is no sign that the tradition created by
the poets of *The Nation* which had inspired so many
young poets in Ireland has influenced the writers represented here." *New Songs,* the editor claimed, reveals
"a new mood in Irish verse," in which "there is no more
echoing of greater voices." He expressed the hope "that
among these new writers are names which may well be
famous hereafter." How accurate was his hopeful pre-
diction? Fame is relative and subject to constant modifi-
cation. Of the eight writers included, Padraic Colum
and Seumas O'Sullivan alone became professional men

of letters, each with a considerable body of fine poetry and other work. Susan Mitchell joined Eva Gore-Booth, Alice Milligan, and Ella Young as minor writers, contributing in small but substantial ways to the Irish Revival.

Similar to Yeats's impressions were those of the young Oliver Gogarty. His review was published in the first issue (May 1904) of the short-lived magazine *Dana,* edited by John Eglinton and Frederick Ryan. *Dana* is perhaps most noteworthy now for its rejection of James Joyce's essay, "A Portrait of the Artist," and for its publication in August 1904 of Joyce's poem, "My love is in a light attire." If we may trust Joyce's brother Stanislaus, it was the rejection of the essay which proved ultimately responsible for the great novel of similar title. Gogarty, like Joyce not included in *New Songs,* found that the volume aroused feelings "indefinite, variegated, confused and beautiful, as if one gazed at a great figured window in an unknown cathedral." Predominant was "a sense of the skill and faultlessness of the verse," and a corresponding "want of fulness of matter, of inspiration." An exception was found by Gogarty, as Yeats had also found, in O'Sullivan's "The Twilight People." Gogarty also joined Yeats in commending Padraic Colum, citing a different poem, "A Drover," for "its great lurching movement." Against such a high standard the reviewer saw for the most part "a perfection which belongs to the conservatory, an artificial perfection."

In the early years of this century Susan Mitchell was

one of those minor figures who could contribute to any occasion, serious or mocking. It was to be expected then, that as a by-product of the riots during the opening week of Synge's "The Playboy of the Western World" a skit should appear, and that Susan Mitchell should be among the contributors. The story is told by Page L. Dickinson, in his reminiscences, *The Dublin of Yesterday* (1929). After the play, he recalls, "somebody suggested writing an account" of the disturbances:

> We did so, and a pamphlet was produced and finished next day which took the form of a parody on the *Arrow*, the journal of the theatre edited by W. B. Yeats. It was illustrated by Richard and William Orpen, and the original cover represented Erin leading an Irish wolfhound: our cover, Mrs. Grundy restraining Synge.

THE ABBEY ROW, NOT Edited by W. B. Yeats is an amusing souvenir of the excitement, both bitter and gay. Susan Mitchell contributed a comic ode on the inflammatory word "shift" which enraged the house when the hero extolled Pegeen with the words, "and what'd I care if you brought me a drift of chosen females, standing in their shifts itself, maybe." Lady Gregory, who had telegraphed Yeats in Scotland, "Play great success," dispatched a second wire, "Audience broke up in disorder at the word shift." The events of the week are familiar to those who know the history of the Abbey Theatre, and can be found in biographies of the principals. Miss Mitchell's verse opens with her characteristic lilt, and a slyly appropriate suggestion of the proper musical setting:

OH, NO! WE NEVER MENTION IT!
(AIR: EARLY VICTORIAN.)

Oh, no, we never mention it, its name is never heard—
New Ireland sets its face against the once familiar word.
They take me to the Gaelic League where men wear kilts,
    and yet
The simple word of childhood's days I'm bidden to forget!

They tell me no one says it now, but yet to give me ease—
If I must speak they bid me use a word that rhymes with
    "sneeze."
But, oh! their cold permission my spirits cannot lift—
I only want the dear old word, the one that ends in " 'ift."

The next year, 1908, saw the publication of two slight volumes, representing both sides of Miss Mitchell's talent, the serious and the light. Seumas O'Sullivan recalls that when the idea of publishing her humorous work was suggested, "she was quite terrified," and it required considerable persuasion before he was able to print, first the *Aids . . .*, and then later in the year, *The Living Chalice,* both of which were issued in enlarged editions five years afterward, in 1913.

2
Aids to the Immortality of Certain Persons in Ireland

They are indeed fortunate who first make the acquaintance of Susan Mitchell through the *Aids to Immortality* in the pamphlet edition of 1908. The cover panel of Irish notables in caricature is a fitting frame for the informal and genial satire of the poems. The sketch by Beatrice Elvery (later Lady Glenavy) focusses upon W. B. Yeats in what must have been a characteristic harangue. With both arms outstretched and head forward, he dominates the group. Behind him is a bewildered Edward Martyn with a childlike expression on his round spectacled face. Yeats is turned to his left. Back of his arm is the lean figure of George Moore, a faint suggestion of a halo above his head. Facing Yeats is the bearded Douglas Hyde, seemingly the only one paying attention to the poet. Isolated in the center is the shambling figure of AE in rumpled suit, hands in pockets. He faces front, apparently unaware of his companions. Of the remaining characters, the dapper Hugh Lane stands out, hat in hand and coat over arm. Here is a frieze of those commemorated in the skits.

The book is furnished with the paraphernalia of pseudo-preface and advertisements which anticipates the modern trends of anti-art. Dedicated to *"MY MOTHER, Whose most fervent prayer for her children was that they might have a sense of humour,"* the text removes all doubt regarding at least one daughter; according to the publisher, the poet and bookman Seumas O'Sullivan, a second daughter, Jane, also lived up to this expectation. The spirit of fun is further carried out by a page of rejected dedications; allusions to characteristic foibles include one to Russell's mysticism:

> Hear a more cheerful poet sing,
> You old, unhappy far-off thing.

and another to Yeats's affectations:

> Oh, he had not these ways
> Ere all the wild mummer was in his gaze.

In providing her own review, the author affords an opportunity to smile at the pretensions of literary criticism and to gibe at the cult of mutual admiration among Irish writers. Yeats had opened his preface to Lady Gregory's *Cuchulain of Muirthemne* (1902) with the triumphant words, "I think this book is the best that has come out of Ireland in my time." Joyce puts this sentence in the mouth of Buck Mulligan in the library chapter of *Ulysses,* but Susan Mitchell had spied the pomposity some dozen years earlier. She begins:

"This is the best book that has come out of Ireland in my time." It is a synthesis of modern Irish history, literature, biography, and Art.

After this promising opening she raises possible objections—"that the jokes are small," or that it is too personal—only to conclude that

Yes, I have written a splendid book. How happy all who are mentioned in it will be. Their fame is secure.

As for those who regret not being included,

I implore them not to be discouraged, everything cannot be said in thirty-seven pages. I may write another book.

To conclude the preliminaries, the "Prologue" is a parody of Yeats's beautiful adaptation of Ronsard, "When you are old and grey and full of sleep," with the mock injunction

> *. . . take down THIS BOOK.*

And think how many people took your part
  Because your works were boomed in some review.
  One woman loved the foolish souls in you
That made you perfect subjects for Her Art.

The volume opens with a three-part ballad history of George Moore, crammed with allusions to his pretentious pronouncements, his continuous monodrama of himself against the Irish people and the Catholic Church. To elucidate the references in these poems would be to footnote the early years of the revival. The first ballad, for instance, has as its title a triple pun.

"Crosses to Ireland" literally refers to the flourish with which Moore returned from London, told in such charmingly vainglorious manner in *Hail and Farewell*. Its secondary meanings are, of course, to the celebrated early Irish stone crosses, and to the tribulations which Moore's presence brought. At one of the early public occasions of the Irish Theatre, Moore extolled the Gaelic Revival, only to conclude anticlimactically that he himself was too old to learn the language, but would urge it upon his nephews. This gives Miss Mitchell her cue:

I've puffed the Irish language, and puffed the Irish soap;
I've used them—on my nephew—with the best results, I hope;

The lampoon continues with Moore recalling:

And so I came to Dublin, and Dublin welcomed me,
For my penitence in paragraphs was very fair to see.

In a more heroic vein:

Jove thunders from Olympus, and Moore from Ely Place,
I damn respectability, and call it a disgrace;

As for the theatre, "We have reformed the Drama, myself and Yeats allied," the others being subject to quick dismissal:

For I took small stock in Martyn, and less in Douglas Hyde;
To bow the knee to rare A.E. was too much for my pride.

But W. B. was the boy for me—he of the dim, wan clothes;
And—don't let on I said it—not above a bit of pose;
And they call his writing literature, as everybody knows.

The second "ballad" (actually, like the first, a poem in triple rhymed stanzas) concerns Moore's loudly heralded apostasy from the Catholic church. It ends, however, with disappointment at the lack of response from the public:

I've had no dramatic moment, I don't even look a fool,
I'm just a Protestant, that's all, they took me very cool.
Come, Georgie—get your Bible, it's time for Sunday School!

When Moore became sheriff in County Mayo, the Dublin literary scene lost a central character, its playboy. The third part of the history of George Moore thus ends with a lament:

We've some bright boys in Ireland, we've got our W. B.
Faith, Martyn, we have got yourself, we've also got A. E.
When Plunkett isn't writing books he is our pride and joy,
And though MacDonnell may be glum, he's not a bad wee boy;
We love our own O'Grady, we love our Douglas Hyde.
And from this pleasant company there's one we won't divide.
'Tis yourself, Moore, you're the playboy, but you're faithful to the green,
Though you're hangin' men and women down in Ballaghadereen,
    Down in Ballaghadereen, down in Ballaghadereen,
    Sending souls to instant glory down in Ballaghadereen.

The irony of the patriot turned squire and sheriff is reinforced by Susan Mitchell's choice of vehicle, the stanza form and meter of the patriotic song, "The Wearing of the Green." The parodist varies the form by adding the two-line refrain. The first stanza of the original concludes:

She's the most distressful country that ever yet was seen,
They are hanging men and women for the wearing of the
  green.

"The Voice of One" caricatures Yeats's domination
of the Irish theatre, and renders absurd his concepts of
poetic drama. Purporting to be a discussion of Bates,
Barton, and M'Clure (Yeats, Martyn, and Moore), it
soon devolves into a soliloquy, in which the enraptured
poet hails his new art:

> A thought I hold by one long gleaming tress,
> A thought of delicate, dim loveliness.
> The Drama of to-morrow draweth nigh,
> I its inventor, its creator I.
> No theatre, no scenery, no stage,
> No clothes the roving fancy to engage,
> No actors either, for their gestures rude
> Break in upon the spirit's solitude.
> And neither shall my plays have any lines—
> The straitened word the wingéd thought confines.

"The ballad of Shawe Taylor and Hugh Lane" takes
the reader into the controversies over the establishment
of a Municipal Gallery for Dublin. The necessary background is provided by Lady Gregory's biography of
Hugh Lane (1921). With a sixth sense for the quality
of unrecognized old masters, Lane, a nephew of Lady
Gregory, had made a series of coups in the art market,
involving paintings by Hals, Cuyp, Rembrandt, Velas-
quez, and others. As a result he was dealing in thousands
of pounds annually when only twenty-three. A chance
visit to Lady Gregory's Coole Park in 1900 marked the
beginning of his conversion to the cause of Irish art. At

first he appeared to Yeats as a man of worldly ambition, with little taste or intelligence: "In my impatience I thought of his knowledge of old pictures as a mere trade knowledge," Yeats recalled. Within a few months, however, Lane's energies turned to the cause of modern art for Ireland, and Yeats sensed a corresponding change in Lane's appearance, an exemplification of the poet's concept of Unity of Being:

> His face and his bodily movements seemed to have changed, they had a curious precision. He had become exceedingly unworldly, contemptuous even of the old lures and perhaps less anxious to please, less agreeable.

Lady Gregory failed to date this reminiscence, but it suggests the image of artistic and aristocratic defiance which preoccupied the later Yeats.

The first of Lane's contributions to Irish art was his commissioning a series of portraits of contemporaries. J. B. Yeats, the poet's father, was encouraged to return from London, and other painters were engaged. The result is that the faces of most Irish leaders at the turn of the century are now familiar. A series of Irish exhibitions was arranged. Gifts from Whistler, Sargent, Rodin and others were promised for a proposed gallery of modern art. In 1904 an unexpected windfall occurred, the possibility of purchasing on special terms the French collection of Mr. Staats Forbes. A selection of 160 of these pictures, together with some borrowed from Durant-Ruel of Paris and about a hundred items already promised by Lane and his friends, opened in November 1904. Jealousy, detraction, and rumor soon arose. Lane was suspected of mercenary motives. Arthur Griffith's nationalistic journal, *The United Irishman,* reflected the current uneasiness and bitterness:

We trust the Municipal Art Gallery will become a reality . . . [but] . . . there is no reason why a ready-made collection of French pictures should be accepted for it. . . . Mr. Moore and his friends allege that the Royal Hibernian Academicians are jealous of the present exhibition in Abbey-street, and are anxious to evict it . . . [fearing] . . . that the familiarisation of the Dublin public with good art will stop the sale of the academicians' annual crop of indifferent canvasses. The academicians, on the other hand, allege that Mr. Hugh Lane is a picture-dealer, and that *they* are the real and unselfish apostles of art. It is a quarrel which, if not unamusing, is squalid. (December 17, 1904)

The editorial concluded on a characteristically chauvinistic note: "If we are to have a creditable Irish school of painting, we shall not create it by slavish imitation of a foreign school."

Yeats demanded a retraction: "I went to the office of the paper, which had till then been a supporter of our movement, and had the most substantial row of my lifetime, and acquired an animosity that will last till my death," as indeed it did. (Gregory, *Hugh Lane* (1921), p. 59) But something of an apology appeared in the next issue, a week later:

We have been assured the inference which might be drawn from a fact we referred to last week—that Mr. Hugh Lane is a professional picture-dealer, would do Mr. Lane injustice. . . . We have been invited to verify the assurance by examining the accounts. It is quite unnecessary. The word of a gentleman is sufficient in such a matter.

The concluding sentence may be a grudging concession to Yeats, in whose account of the affair, quoted by Lady Gregory, the unnamed editor remained stubbornly opposed to that very principle. Griffith is reported to have said that trusting those who presumed to be gentlemen would soon wreck the country. (*Hugh Lane,* p. 60)

A long preface this, to the occasion of Miss Mitchell's amusing poem. In May 1905 the Municipal Collection was exhibited at the National Museum of Ireland; well over a hundred works of art had been acquired by gift and purchase. But the director of the Museum, Lieutenant-Colonel G. T. Plunkett, who oddly enough held office under the sanction of the Department of Agriculture and Technical Instruction, was jealous of Lane, and he expressed his animosity by displaying photographs which purported to throw doubt upon the authenticity of an early Corot, purchased from the Staats Forbes estate. An almost identical landscape, though twenty times the size of the small Corot, was discovered in the Budapest Museum. It was painted after Corot's death by the Hungarian, Géza Mészöly (1844–87). The implication of fraud was apparent, whether Lane be perpetrator or victim. As Thomas Bodkin tells the story in his *Hugh Lane and his Pictures* (1932),

> The gallant Colonel did this without Lane's knowledge, during his absence, and created the outcry he desired. But in the midst of his triumph, Lane's cousin, Captain Shawe-Taylor, entered the Museum with a turnscrew, explained the true inwardness of the situation to the sympathetic policemen on guard, and removed the offending photographs, which he carried away under his arm.

Mr. Bodkin recalls that "The incident furnished Susan

Mitchell with material for a delicious comic ballad,
which she sang herself, in a pleasant throaty voice, at
many gatherings in Dublin drawing-rooms and studios."

Shawe-Taylor, it should be remembered, was also a
nephew of Lady Gregory, and the subject of a brief
prose eulogy by Yeats, who characterized him as still
another instance of Unity of Being: "whose good looks
are the image of their faculty; and these men, copying
hawk or leopard, have an energy of swift decision, a
power of sudden action, as if their whole body were
their brain."

"The Ballad of Shawe-Taylor and Hugh Lane" com-
prises a vignette of the Irish scene worthy of extended
quotation:

> UP spake our brave Shaw[e] Taylor—
> That Captain wise and great—
> "To every Irishman on earth
> Arrest comes soon or late,
> And how can man do better
> Than suffer grief and pain
> For the glory of Apollo
> And his servant, Hugh P. Lane?["]
>
> And so to the Museum
> He marched with gallant air,
> With his good turnscrew by his side
> He climbed the echoing stair;
> Under the portly peeler's nose
> He gave a fatal twist,
> Wrenched off that odious photograph
> With one turn of the wrist.
>
> The peeler, who'd been thinking hard,
> And thus felt ill at ease,
> Now to Shawe Taylor did advance

And said, "Sir, if you please,
You have been guilty of offence
Against the law, and so
You must put on the handcuffs
And to Kilmainham go."

But the Captain's eloquent voice prevailed, and he left
the museum to confront "Dublin's best and wittiest"
who had gathered to gaze upon the hero:

A.E. was there with his long hair,
And Orpen, R.H.A.,
Sir Thomas Drew was in a stew,
And looked the other way,
But Martyn, who had left the stage
To play the patriot's part,
Called for Hungarian policy
In everything but art!

And John B. Yeats stood near the gates
With mischief in his gaze,
While W. B., the poet, he
Pondered a telling phrase,
You'll find it in the *Freeman*
After a day or so.
And Moore was there—the same who is
High Sheriff for Mayo
. . . .

So let us hymn Apollo,
And hymn Shawe Taylor too,
For if the picture's Corot's
We think it cheap, don't you?
And if the picture's Mezoly's [*sic*]
Our policy's Sinn Féin,
And the glory's still Apollo's
And his servant, Hugh P. Lane!

The basic topical irony is that the offending artist
was Hungarian, and that Griffith, whose ambivalent at-

titude we have examined, had derived his "Hungarian policy" from the winning of quasi-independence by Hungary in the establishment of the dual monarchy of Austria-Hungary, as outlined in his articles, later collected in a booklet entitled *The Resurrection of Hungary* (1904). Orpen was the fashionable painter William Orpen (1878–1931); Sir Thomas Drew, architect of the National Museum and the flanking National Library, was one who opposed Hugh Lane's projects. We can recognize the mischief in the eyes of J. B. Yeats from his self portrait, reproduced as the frontispiece of *J. B. Yeats, Letters to His Son W. B. Yeats and Others, 1869–1922* (1944). W.B.'s propensity for carrying disputes to the press is suggested, and, of course, "Moore was there," Miss Mitchell's favorite target. Moore had, in fact, lectured on "Reminiscences of the Impressionist Painters," during the exhibition of 1904, and thus deserved better treatment than he is afforded in Miss Mitchell's ballad.

"The Irish Council Bill, 1907" celebrates the failure of a diluted half-way step towards Home Rule, an attempt, in the words of Éoin O'Mahony, "to kill Home Rule by kindness." It proposed an administrative council of 106 members, only 82 of whom were to be elected. Its defeat by an Irish convention, which regarded it as a shabby compromise of the Liberal promise of Home Rule, ensured the failure of the Irish Parliamentary Party and paved the way for the Sinn Fein victories a decade later. The poem, a light-hearted jingle, opens:

> Is it this you call Home Rule?
> Says the Shan Van Vocht.

> Do you take me for a fool?
>   Says the Shan Van Vocht.
> To be sending round the hat
> Five-and-twenty years for that
> Isn't good enough for Pat,
>   Says the Shan Van Vocht.

The verse form is that of the popular anonymous song about the attempted French invasion of 1796, "The Shan Van Vocht" (poor old woman; i.e., Ireland), beginning "Oh! the French are on the sea."

The 1908 edition concludes with its most successful poem, a parody of Kipling's "Recessional." Kipling, as apologist for Empire, was fair game for Irish nationalists:

ODE TO THE BRITISH EMPIRE
DEDICATED TO THE ARCHBISHOPS
AND BISHOPS OF THE CHURCH OF IRELAND

> GOD of the Irish Protestant,
>   Lord of our proud Ascendancy,
> Soon there'll be none of us extant,
>   We want a few plain words with thee.
>   Thou know'st our hearts are always set
>   On what we get, on what we get.

The lament continues, as "The landlords with the bonus fly," leaving no more gold upon the offering plate. "Off went each fat emolument" with the elimination of tithes and establishment:

> Now one by one of each asset
> You've robbed us, this we can't forget.

Revenge upon all is the tenor of the conclusion, which alas, was to prove prophetic:

> God of the Irish Protestant,
>   You have grown hideous in our sight;
> You're not the kind of god we want.
>   Rise, Sons of William, rise and smite!
>   New gods we'll serve, and with them yet
>   We'll get all there is left to get!

It is worthy of remark that Susan Mitchell herself was a Protestant. Seumas O'Sullivan quotes a letter of hers which discusses this "ode," and reiterates her espousal of it: "Satires are Satires, and my Ode fits in perfectly. . . . And I am not going to change it." "The Mitchells have been Protestants since Luther and probably long before," she continues, while she promises to "please all parties" by writing "a Catholic Song to match my Ode—I have always recognised the Catholics to be weaker vessels and spared them." Later she confessed that though she had "written verses on verses" (two stanzas survive in the Armagh notebook) the promised song would not come; "I know my own church, and better the devil I know than the devil I don't know."

In keeping with the playful fooling of the volume is the page of publisher's announcements of autumn titles by "Wellsell and Co." (Maunsel). These include a sequel to Yeats's *Ideas of Good and Evil,* namely *No Ideas Good or Bad,* a treatise by AE on *Supernatural Law in the Economic World,* a genial gibe at Russell's mixture of mystical and economic thought, and sermons by the bachelor Edward Martyn entitled *Women of No Importance.*

Among her victims, at least AE and Yeats bore her no ill will. AE's tribute has already been quoted. As for Yeats, I have in my possession a holograph parody of his "Lake Isle of Innsfree", intended as a thank-you poem, with accompanying postcard, apparently delivered to the painter Susan Purser by Yeats himself, since the poem has *"per W. B. Y."* under the autographed text, and the postcard to Miss Purser is unstamped. First, the card:

Wednesday

You are awfully good to me—You are just a gem—and I must get the hat—& be as smart as I can. How do you like the other side, taken while singing in AE's back garden. There is rhyme, but I don't know if there's reason!

The parody, signed, on an 8″ by 10½″ sheet, reads:

I will arise & run now and run to Grafton Street
And a fine bonnet buy there with fur & feathers great
Bright hatpins I shall place there, put spats on my twinkling
   feet,
And walk like a fashion plate.

And I will have some joy there for vanity will blaze
Blazing from the brown eyes to the feet that go to & fro
And my ears will be cocked to listen [to] the whisper of
   young men's praise

And my heart will be all aglow

I will arise & go now for always night & day
I want to hear the praise of the world rise up into a roar
And when it reaches crescendo your "vain little piece" will
   pray
For you in her deep heart's core!

Susan L. Mitchell
per W. B. Y.

The photograph on the postcard shows the author standing, half-length, bare-headed, wearing an open

jacket over a white high-collar shirtwaist, a locket round
her neck. The costume could be dated approximately
1910. Beside the photograph is a printed Christmas
greeting, which is interesting as a light-hearted apologia
for her art:

> Come gather round me neighbours, and
>   listen while I tell,
> How I sang of bards and peelers, not
>   wisely but too well;
> 'Till some said I was a Fenian, and some
>   a Unionist,
> And still I went on singing, I couldn't
>   hould my whisht.
> You know my little foolish songs—but,
>   please, don't take it ill,
> If I wish you a merry Xmas—and go on
>   singing still.

She did go on singing still. Robin Skelton reported an
additional stanza of "The Irish Council Bill," written
in pencil and signed "Susan," in his own copy of the
1908 edition of *Aids to the Immortality of Certain Persons in Ireland*. It is headed "April 1910," but was not
printed in the second edition of that work. The stanza
concludes:

> *Budgets four we've had since then*
> *And we still are asking—When?*
> *God Almighty, give us* men
>   *Says the Shan Van Vocht*
>   ("Susan L. Mitchell: An Unrecorded
>   Item," *The Irish Book* I, #4 (Spring
>   1962), p. 104)

The second edition (1913) is considerably enlarged,

but not always improved. Gone is the cover panel, in favor of a simulated half-vellum binding, uniform with the second and final edition of *The Living Chalice,* published in the same year. Gone are the rejected dedications; the "Author's Review" is enlarged, made more explicit, and less subtle. She opens with her statement of purpose:

> FOR the writer who has no critical faculty, the ordinary commercial reviewer may be good enough, but when one is exceptionally gifted, as I am, with both the critical and creative faculty, why should he wait for any middle interest, like reviewing, to wriggle in between him and his victim the public, before he has had time to grip it by the throat.

Since "this may be the best review I will get," she promises to "be frank and above-board" and to "discount all your objections beforehand." First, "There is too much George Moore in it." Carried away by her obsession with, or rather against, Moore, she quotes several paragraphs from her review of *Ave,* which is, indeed too much Moore. Once she has dismissed Moore, she hurries to her conclusion. The second criticism— "too impartial and too flippant"—is brushed aside, and she closes with praise for her own technique as "nearly perfect," since she admits to being "an adept at rhyming," and she has handled well her medium, personalities.

The enlarged edition lacks the neat unity of the much shorter early collection, with its triple ballad on Moore, followed by the two poems on the arts in Dublin—theatre and painting—and concluding with two political pieces. Perhaps because she has added other satires on Moore, she breaks up the "Ballad History," placing the second and third parts later. The magnificent finale of the first volume is almost lost between these satires of Moore. Another political piece comes as an appropriate addendum to the Irish Council poem. This, "The Black-thorn Convention," commemorates the founding of the All For Ireland League by two disaffected leaders of the Parliamentary Party, Tim Healy and William O'Brien. With their slogan of "Conference, Conciliation, and Consent" they won eight seats in January 1910, and others in later elections, thus splitting the Parliamentary Party and preparing for the Sinn Fein victories of 1917 and 1918. P. S. O'Hegarty comments, in *A History of Ireland Under the Union, 1801–1922* (1952) that though John Redmond kept the majority, "O'Brien and Healy were always just after forming a new party or just after uniting with the old." Susan Mitchell's poem is largely a lament by the erstwhile uncontested leader, Redmond:

> JOHN REDMOND spake up boldly:
> 'My members, every day
> The people look more coldly
> On everything we say.
> My gift for making speeches
> Is rusting with disuse,
> Sinn Feiners with their screeches
> Will send us to the deuce.'

Susan Mitchell's political sympathies were far more extreme than those of most of her associates. She became a member of the Sinn Fein independence group at an unusually early date, and her targets were members of the Parliamentary Party who are jokingly accused of compromising for the sake of expediency. The party, it must be recognized, had been weakened by the split over Parnell, and in the ensuing years there emerged almost every shade of opinion, much of it impractical by the very nature of things. "Nursery Rhymes for Co-Operative Babes," to the meter of "A Frog He Would a Wooing Go," describes John Dillon's attack on Horace Plunkett's scheme of cooperative marketing; the organ of Plunkett's Irish Agricultural Organisation Society was *The Irish Homestead*, which employed AE and Susan Mitchell. Dillon, whose policy is described as "Damn Co-operation for the Irish nation," enlists the aid of T. W. Russell, head of the Department of Agriculture for Ireland, urging him to eliminate Plunkett. "Says Russell, going back on my Party's a strain," to which Dillon rejoins, "But you did it before, you can do it again." Russell agrees, promising to name a committee of "the tried and the true." Though she was not a political ally of Plunkett,* she supported the cooperative movement, and concludes her poem with editorializing:

> Oh damn it, why can't ye be sportsmen, say we,
> Get Co-operation for the Irish nation, get some
> Sense for yourself, Mr. Dillon.

* Sir Horace Plunkett, incidentally, is one of a confusing number of men of that name prominent in Ireland at the time—Lieutenant-Colonel G. T., Director of the National Museum; Edward, the playwright Lord Dunsany; George Noble, a Papal Count, first to be elected to Parliament on the Sinn Fein ticket in 1917; and his son, Joseph Mary, poet, executed by the British for his part in the 1916 Rising. As for the Russells, in addition to George William, the poet AE, there were the above mentioned T. W., Father Matthew, S. J., editor of the *Irish Monthly*, and George William Erskine, an early friend of Sir Horace Plunkett.

The plight of the Irish Agricultural Organisation Society is the subject of a long letter by AE to the Right Honourable A. J. Balfour, under date of January 23, 1913. Similar societies had been granted funds in England and Scotland, but the Irish grant had been delayed on two grounds, political and economic. The I.A.O.S. was, according to AE's letter, accused of being "a device of Sir Horace Plunkett's to upset the Home Rule cause," the charge being based on an injudicious remark made in a letter by T. W. Rolleston, one of the founders of the Irish Literary Society. The letter, published in the *Freeman's Journal*, opined "that the I.A.O.S. would get rid of Dillon and the Parliamentarians." The letter, AE explained, led to Russell's animosity toward the organization, despite Rolleston's assertion that his statement was merely a personal opinion. AE concluded by pointing out that the I.A.O.S. was the only Irish movement "which has succeeded in uniting Catholic and Protestant, Unionist and Nationalist in a common object."

Two poems relevant to the "Playboy" disturbances are included. First, "The Playboy" amusingly alludes to the fallacy of considering a work of imagination a slur upon an author's country. In each stanza a great national literature is thus rejected. Since *Oedipus Rex* depicts "a Greek who killed his da," the conclusion is inevitable:

> I know now Plato was a sham,
>   And Socrates I brush aside,
> For Phidias I don't give a damn,
>   For every Greek's a parricide!

Shakespeare was no better:

> The character of Falstaff shows
> In Merrie England's every son—
> Bullies and yet afraid of blows,
> Drunkards and gluttons every one.

With the result that Asquith and Balfour, the two most prominent contemporary English political leaders—and the men most closely watched by the Home Rulers!—must be discarded: "The Falstaff in them all I see." Here the paradox comes amusingly close to truth. Germany, whose Faust is scarcely a model, and France, with Moliere and Voltaire, also go by the boards, while Italy, "In spite of its cathedral bells," is suspect, since Dante showed acquaintance with "far too many hells." The poem concludes:

> Have playwrights left me any land
> That's fit for my white feet to tread,
> Where dull and decent I may stand,
> And, yawning, wish that I were dead?

Next comes "Oh No! We Never Mention It," from *The Abbey Row.*

The remaining poems, almost all political, are less successful, because the author relies heavily on contemporary allusions to such now-forgotten names as Dermody, Hynes, or John Cotton. In Miss Mitchell's verse they often remain merely names, because their own characters are not developed. Comparison with Alexander Pope is instructive. Historical identification is scarcely necessary for the appreciation of his art. His dull poetasters, his nouveaux riches, his gluttons and parasites are sharply though cruelly drawn, their specific vices underscored. "Search then the RULING PASSION," he urges, since "This clue once found, unravels all the rest." As one example, in the fourth of Pope's "Moral Essays," concerning the use of riches, the vulgarity of Timon's villa, reeking with false magnificence, is plain to see, regardless of whose estate was depicted:

> At Timon's Villa let us pass a day,
> Where all cry out, "What sums are thrown away!"
> So proud, so grand; of that stupendous air,
> Soft and Agreeable come never there.
> Greatness, with Timon, dwells in such a draught
> As brings all Brobdignag before your thought.
> To compass this, his building is a Town,
> His pond an Ocean, his parterre a Down:
> Who but must laugh, the Master when he sees,
> A puny insect, shivering at a breeze!
> Lo, what huge heaps of littleness around!
> The whole, a laboured Quarry above ground;
>
> (99–110)

And on the unwilling guest goes, through a mechanically symmetrical landscape ("Grove nods at grove, each Alley has a brother") to the chapel where "the Pride of Prayer" is celebrated beneath painted ceilings with "Light quirks of music." The full scene is there.

Few satirists can be compared with Pope, Swift, or Dryden, but Susan Mitchell does have the talent to hit her targets. Robin Skelton puts the matter well in his brief but penetrating essay, "Aide to Immortality," in *The World of W. B. Yeats,* edited by Robin Skelton and Ann Saddlemyer (1965). He finds her a "lampoon-ist rather than a satirist; her best jokes are both local and ephemeral, but on occasion she can wield the weapon of parody with some force." He points out that though many of her parodies now seem merely enter-taining, and despite the lack of the urbanity and sub-tlety of the great satirist,

> It is clear that Susan Mitchell intended her lampoons to act with maximum efficiency in a particular situation, and did not expect them to interest posterity. As a conse-quence her work is now largely forgotten, but, when re-discovered, brings back the feel of her times more strongly than the work of many of her more distinguished con-temporaries. (pp. 236–237)

The "Anti-Recruiting Song" fails for other reasons; the eager recruit who becomes a pathetic gull of the military system is hardly an original conception, nor is this lad sufficiently identified to make the obvious conclusion poignant. Perhaps in an attempt to avoid sentimentality, or possibly because of her facility in the meter, an unfortunate jingling effect is achieved, as in the opening lines:

He took the English shilling, his Bible oath he swore,
To serve the King of England. He left the Shannon shore.

There are two additional George Moore poems, neither of them so memorable as the three of the ballad history. His gastronomic taste is commemorated in the refrain, "The fish I left behind me," that is, the grey mullet at Henri's French restaurant:

Ah! what a hero-heart I gave
        Without a thought of fooling,
To live in Dublin and to brave
        Bad cooks and English ruling.
But could I feed as once I fed,
        Regret should never find me,
For *Ave atque Vale* said
        To the fish I left behind me.

Here the principal value is that of the recognized source. A poem less familiar to American readers than "The Girl I Left Behind Me" is the sing-song Percy French "The Queen's Afterdinner Speech," itself a parody of mechanical Gaelic meters. The song writer characterizes his work "As Overheard and Cut into Lengths of Poetry by Jamesy Murphy, Deputy-Assistant-Waiter at the Viceregal Lodge." Its occasion was the royal visit of April 1900, which had aroused protests from many Dubliners. Percy French has the queen reflect on

". . . that other wan," sez she,
"That Maud Gonne," sez she,
"Dhressin' in black," sez she,
"To welcome me back," sez she,

And as for Willie Yeats,

"He should be at home," sez she,
"French polishin' a pome," sez she,
"An' not writin' letters," sez she,
"About his betters," sez she,

From which it may be inferred that there were other accomplished writers of satirical verse at the time.

Miss Mitchell's opening stanza of "George Moore

Becomes the Priest of Aphrodite" achieves an extraor-
dinarily conversational tone within such a repetitious
pattern:

> In good Victoria's humdrum days
>   I started my career, Sir,
> I from Mayo to France did go,
>   Where I acted very queer, Sir.
> But I my sins repenting sore,
>   To pious Dublin came, Sir,
> And though I find most things a bore,
>   I stay here all the same, Sir.
> But if you ask me to explain,
>   I really cannot say, Sir,
> Why I in Dublin still remain
>   When I might go away, Sir.

As for his much vaunted turn to Protestantism, "my
views on Saving Grace/ The Puritans found flighty,"
with an unusual outcome:

> Behold me now in Ely Place
>   The priest of Aphrodite.

However,

> . . . even this does not explain,
>   Nor can I really say, Sir,
> Why I in Dublin still remain
>   When I might go away, Sir.

The "Ballad of Dermody and Hynes" rises to a peak
of bitter eloquence in its characterization of the Irish.
The tale of a miscarriage of justice, "one law for the
people and one for the police," has as its envoy a muffled
call to arms:

We are a pleasant people, the laugh upon our lip
Gives answer back to your laugh in gay good fellowship;
We dance unto your piping, we weep when you want tears;
Wear a clown's dress to please you, and to your friendly jeers
Turn up a broad fool's face and wave a flag of green—
But the naked heart of Ireland, who, who has ever seen?

Irish hearts, like Irish sword-blades, were last bared in
the Rising of 1798, and have since been sheathed, as
Parnell and Mitchel wished— a sad eventuality:

Ah, bitter sheathing! now we wave a foolish flag of green,
And measure wits with peelers, and take ashplants and drive
Dumb cattle like ourselves—good God, are we alive?

"Lines on a Threatened Imperial University" warn
of the danger that the native tongue may be lost through
English control of education; "The Rival Clubs," with
echoes of the "Walrus and the Carpenter," depicts the
struggle in the soul of Cotton (William Cotton, Lord
Mayor of Dublin) as he is torn between his patriot
scruples and the genteel life of the Ascendancy:

'Oh, Cotton, come and join our club,' the Tories did
    beseech;
'With many a lord and baronet you shall have daily speech,
A chair in a warm corner; lunches—a shilling each.'

The Irish leader of the Parliamentary Party, Johnny
Redmond, finally reconciles "The love of Peer and
People in William Cotton's soul," with the prospect of
an abolition of the House of Lords. His last scruple
"he swallowed whole" and "Not one conviction had he
when he came unto the poll."

Of the anti-Ulster poems which reflect the rising

tensions between Northern and Southern Ireland on the eve of a long-promised Home Rule Bill the most successful is the savage mockery of the "Ode to Bluff," with its invocation:

> O HEAVENLY Bluff descend on us,
> God that each Ulsterman inspires,
> Wake unto speech each timid cuss,
> And make us sounding liars.

Pun, parody, and caricature mark the description of the militant Ulster leader Carson:

> Make us thy lyres even as Carson is.
> Let us lay down our lives as he lays his.

Sir Edward Carson doubles as Noah in the satiric lampoon, "The Ark of the Covenant." In protest against Home Rule, Carson and other Ulster leaders had drawn up a Covenant, reminiscent of their Scottish forebears, who in 1557, 1581, and in 1638 had pledged support to the Reformed Church. The 1912 Covenant was proclaimed with all the fanfare of a national holiday, with flags flying and special religious services. It defied Home Rule, agreeing "in using all means which may be found necessary to defeat the present conspiracy," and further, "in the event of such a Parliament being forced upon us, we further solemnly and mutually pledge ourselves to refuse to recognize its authority." The petition was signed by more than 219,000 men, who three months later, in December, were called upon to enroll in the citizen army, the Ulster Volunteers. The tensions of those days, like the reactions against civil rights legislation in the United States, remain unabated to the present day.

The poem opens with a depiction of the alarm felt in Ulster:

They wept on every platform, they shed the wettest tears,
And for the lonely Protestant expressed the loudest fears;

Visions of Smithfield massacres were mingled with scorn for the Protestants in the Southern Counties:

'Those southern fools of Protestants defiled themselves with pitch
Instead of settling in Belfast where they'd be saved and rich.'

Following Biblical precedent,

. . . Noah Carson launched his ark, bade Ulster hurry in
And shut the gates upon a land of Popery and sin;—
Their altruistic sentiments gave way to love of pelf,
And Ulster signed the Covenant and swore to save—itself.

Amusingly ironic is "The Kiss," which observes that the long-standing privilege enjoyed by King and Viceroy of kissing debutantes at Court Presentations was abolished by King Edward. The irony is that the king's private life was a matter of public knowledge, and that any puritanical gesture from him was an ultimate hypocrisy. The song-like opening is countered by the innuendo of the conclusion. The poem begins:

The kiss that once through Christendom
    A kindly feeling shed,
Is now for relatives or those

Towards matrimony led.
A universal custom once
Enjoinéd by St. Paul,
It's come to this, the girls won't kiss,
They will not kiss at all.

At the Dublin Castle,

Lord Aberdeen's no longer seen
To give that courtier's kiss
So soothing to the trembling nerves
Of new-presented miss.

The final stanza insinuates the point:

Better the gay song of the kiss,
Its melody and grace,
Than it should like a serpent hiss
In secret shamèd place
Where we have made a darkness
About love's heavenly face.

3

The Living Chalice

Susan Mitchell's serious verse is slight in volume, and one might be excused in thinking it equally slight in content, yet such a judgment would not be entirely fair. Her themes are those of traditional religious dedication, in which the central tension is that between natural and supernatural allegiances. In diction, imagery, and meter the verse is little more than competent, with frequent lapses in rhythm, and a too easy acceptance of the sentimental or commonplace. Yet closer examination will disclose qualities overlooked in such an unfavorable view. As she enlarged the number of poems from the twenty-four in the Tower Press edition of 1908, almost doubling the total for the small vellum-backed hardcover book five years later, it became apparent that the work represented a personal *via crucis*, a suite expressing the sometimes despairing path of a believer toward a firmer faith. Though lacking the brilliant metaphysical daring of George Herbert or

Emily Dickinson, those greater poets may be distantly recalled, as in "The Heart's Low Door":

> O EARTH, I will have none of thee.
>   Alien to me the lonely plain,
> And the rough passion of the sea
>   Storms my unheeding heart in vain.
>
> The petulance of rain and wind
>   The haughty mountains' superb scorn,
> Are but slight things I've flung behind,
>   Old garments that I have out-worn.
>
> Bare of the grudging grass, and bare
>   Of the tall forest's careless shade,
> Deserter from thee, Earth, I dare
>   See all thy phantom brightness fade.
>
> And, darkening to the sun, I go
>   To enter by the heart's low door,
> And find where Love's red embers glow
>   A home, who ne'er had home before.

An art so fragile can easily be underestimated, for the subtle surprises of "petulant" weather, "grudging grass," and "careless shade" are modulated into a context of now unfashionable poetic diction. What saves this verse from banality are these few subtle touches and the paradox, mild rather than bold, of the conclusion, wherein the darkness discloses a hitherto unexpected light.

To compare the two versions of this book is to discover some interesting principles of arrangement and elaboration. The poignant dedication in the first printing was apparently deemed too personal to head the later work; it was wisely placed near the conclusion, and the book begins instead with an evocation of the "monstrous travail" from which life and nature emerge. The volume proper opens with the title poem, "The Living Chalice," forming an introduction to the theme of religious dedication, and, with the next two poems, comprising a group which could be entitled "Initiation." In the first of these, both "Bridegroom's Feast" and "Feast of Life" have remained untouched; the opening stanzas conclude with the wistful refrain, "Master of Life, Thy Cup has passed me by." A third time, however, the feast is set within the soul itself, and consummation is achieved. The imagery is truly metaphysical, with heart and veins constituting a tree of life and cup of sacrifice:

> Eyes of the Soul, awake, awake and see
> Growing within the Ruby Radiant Tree,
> Sharp pain hath wrung the Clusters of my Vine;
> My heart is rose-red with its brimmèd wine.
> Thou hast new-set the Feast and I draw nigh—
> Master of Life take me, thy Cup am I.

The author's shaping imagination in creating her suite of poems can be demonstrated through a detailed comparison of the two editions. Here at the beginning it is shown by her insertion of a new poem, "The Burden of the Doorkeeper." The added poem describes the stern but vaguely defined guardians who preside over the "newly born" and the "newly dead" (a striking anticipation of the enigmatic doorkeeper in Kafka's *The Trial*). Thus for a moment the reader's attention shifts from the initiate of "The Living Chalice," to return once more with "A Prayer," in which she pleads,

as human being and poet alike, for a voice appropriate
to the solemn occasion:

> They need a kingly speech who take
> The lordly pathways of the dead.

This note of lofty solemnity is struck in the next
poem, "Immortality," a poem which AE selected to
illustrate the poet's transcendental imagination when
he reviewed her work after her death. It is a state of
immortal illumination which she attempts to embody
in the invocation:

> AGE cannot reach me where the veils of God
>   Have shut me in,
> For me the myriad births of stars and suns
>   Do but begin,
> And here how fragrantly there blows to me
>   The holy breath,
> Sweet from the flowers and stars and hearts of men,
>   From life and death.

For a moment a true intimation of immortality is
achieved:

> We are not old, O heart, we are not old,
>   The breath that blows
> The soul aflame is still a wandering wind
>   That comes and goes;
> And the stirred heart with sudden raptured life
>   A moment glows.

Yet the mood cannot last; "a child drowned and a heart /
Quickened with pain" intrude, and will not be forgotten. The poem concludes, however, with a note of
triumph:

> We know them not, O happy heart,
>   For you and I
> Watch where within a slow dawn lightens up
>   Another sky.

Two new poems follow, in which the pangs of earthly loss are probed in different directions. "Carrick" depicts an imagined retreat to a land of youth where "sleep is sweet in Carrick town." But the dream is shattered by awareness that those so vividly remembered cannot return:

> O Death, how did you find the way
> You tread so certainly to-day?

The concluding lines suggest Dylan Thomas's use of the small Welsh town as symbol of affectionate reminiscence:

> There are no children on the shore,
> The singing voices sing no more,
> The sea draws all her rivers down,
> And love has sailed from Carrick town.

Constant emphasis on the supernal experience can lead to monotony, for such experience is, in the end, an ineffable and unutterable one. Susan Mitchell does provide some measure of variety, however, in her handling of the inherent contrast between the worldly and the supernatural. A poem based on Christ's suffering, "Light of Lights," contrasts the agony of that first Good Friday, relived by the devout, with the glory of the resurrected Christ. A shadow clouds His face, until He sees, in the smiles of two friends, the sign of those about to be chosen, though in the conflict of temporal and eternal values He, in selecting them to share in His glory, "Knew not men wept more when these died."

Contrast and paradox inform most of the remaining poems, revolt alternating with acceptance. Resistance to an almost unbearable commitment finds utterance in the first line of "The Army of the Voice," with its heartrending cry, "You cannot take me, ah, I will not go." The turmoil of departure brings one to "The tides and surges of your savage sea." The heart in its agony, its wings broken, has "lived in the low valley far too long" and hence

> Can give no echo to your tireless song,
> Voice of God's armies jubilant and strong.

"Loneliness" presents another metaphor of the human condition. Although "They lift me up" and "set a crown on me," the heart remains cold and dry, for "Without thy crowning, love, I am uncrowned."

Subdued modulations of tone give way to more marked changes with three national poems, "Daughters of Erin," "Ireland," and an adaptation from ancient Irish literature, "Amergin." The patriotic poems do not give the effect of an intrusion, however, because of the cardinal theme in the Celtic Revival of identifying innate Irish spirituality with the Hebraic-Christian tradition. The lowly majesty of the native Irish was often equated with the position of the despised and neglected in the Bible. One memorable instance is that of John F. Taylor's speech, quoted in the newsroom chapter of *Ulysses*.

A charming evocation of the Irish countryside is "The Greenlands." The location is at Rosses Point, in Sligo Bay, in the heart of the Yeats country, where Susan Mitchell spent some of her childhood. North is Lissadell, background of the Yeats poem, "In Memory of Eva Gore-Booth and Con Markievicz." Inland is the town of Sligo and the towering cliff of Ben Bulben, seen by Miss Mitchell in the poem "as a god, amethyst and flame," with the colors of the sunset on its bare sides. In her childhood, she recalls:

From every leaf and blade of grass an old sweet wisdom
    came,
And in my heart strange flowers sprang up with every
    hurrying breath. . . .

Now, long after her departure from this almost legendary land of her youth, the countryside appears in a dream:

My soul stole to the Greenlands all in a dream one night,
I saw them stretching wide and fair up to the gates of gold.
I saw my thoughts in quiet flocks move upwards to the light,
And I, their shepherd, went with them to an eternal fold.

"Amergin," considered to be the earliest Irish poem, was supposedly uttered by a Milesian invader, centuries before Christ.

A comparison of several versions serves to define the quality of Susan Mitchell's imagination. First, the opening of Douglas Hyde's:

I am the wind which breathes upon the sea,
I am the wave of the ocean,

I am the murmer of the billows,
I am the ox of the seven combats. . . .

The "I" is later identified with "a word of science,"
"the point of the lance," and finally with "the God who
created in the head the fire."

A more romantic elaboration is included in Dr.
George Sigerson's anthology, *Bards of the Gael and Gall*
(1897). The translator is unidentified; the direct opening resembles that of Douglas Hyde, but is even more
abrupt in tone:

> I, the Wind at Sea,
> I, the rolling Billow,
> I, the roar of Ocean,

which scarcely prepares one for the almost Swinburnian
rhythms of

> I, the Spear for smiting Foemen,
> I, the God for forming Fortune!
> Whither wend by glen or mountain?
> Whither tend beneath the Sunset?
> Whither wander seeking safety?

In place of Douglas Hyde's brief conclusion, a rhetorical
question answered, we have elaboration. Hyde's last
two lines read:

> Who teaches the place where couches the sun?
> (If not I)

This riddle-like wit is Victorianized to

> I, the poet, prophet, pray'rful,
> Weapons wield for warriors' slaying:

Tell of triumph, laud forthcoming
Future fame in soaring story!

According to Douglas Hyde's *A Literary History of Ireland* (1899) the invasion by the sons of Milesius has been dated variously between the eighth century B.C. and 1700 B.C. One could hardly expect accuracy in such matters, but there is a more profound question as to how these verses are to be understood. They seem to represent a pantheistic identification with the forces of nature, but a convincing argument has been made by Alwyn and Brinley Rees (*Celtic Heritage*, 1961) that the verse, with early Indian parallels, is "in the nature of creation incantations" by "the cosmic juggler or magician." On the other hand, Dr. George Sigerson, in his anthology, *Bards of the Gael and Gall* (1897) suggests that this is a "vaunting song" like one of Cuchulainn's, which "uses similar expressions" together "with others which are unmistakably personal vaunts—not pantheistic, but panegoistic." Some support for this interpretation might be found in Dr. Hyde's glossing of the hero's name as "Miledh Easpáin" or "the Champion of Spain."

With this background we may appreciate the playful fantasy with which Susan Mitchell adapts the lines. There is more of Puck than hero or seer in her reading:

I BUZZ in the dizzy fly, I crawl in the creeping things.
I croak in the frog's throat and fly on the bird's wings.

I play on the keys of the brain, a thought goes here, goes
  there;
Bird or beast it has bounds; but I am everywhere.

I dip in the pools of the rocks and the minnow plays
   with me.
Finned I am like a fish, and merry children are we.

And so it dances on for two more stanzas, a lighter poem
than its original certainly, but having a charm of its
own.

In a manner suggestive of Emily Dickinson, spiritual
crises are given homely, domestic metaphors. Religious
yearning is personified as "Love's Mendicant," begging
nothing less than "The Hidden One in thee." "The
Extravagant Heart" attempts without success to escape
the inevitable, failing to realize that however much
time it devour, it remains in want. "The Music of the
Silence" pleads for the soul's release from the bewilder-
ing discords of worldly concern in order to hear the
"perfect melody" within. These dramas of religious
commitment are pleasantly varied with such a playful
bit as the apostrophe to "The Age of Time," whose
"little ways" deceive man, or the paradox regarding the
heart, hospitable to sin, sorrow and anger, healed in
"The Nursery of the Heart." The lot of mankind is to
find oneself "Homeless," his refuge destroyed. "Exile,"
the poem which concluded the first printing, depicts
the wavering flight of the soul, "Thy homeless bird":

> For ever lonely must I go
> From every shelter riven,
> Wing-weary under heaven.

The inevitability of sorrow in life, since love exacts
its own cost of suffering, is given poignant utterance
in the eight Christmas poems which form the coda of

the enlarged edition. The irony is implicit in "Thorns of the Holly," in which the traditional trappings of the holiday season are reminders of love and loss:

> The red-berried holly
>> We set up long ago,
> In tenderest folly
>> We hung the mistletoe.
> Thorns of old affection,
>> Ye pierced us through and through,
> Each year in recollection
>> We pierce ourselves anew.

"The Descent of the Child" reiterates the often felt thought that Christmas is truly the children's holiday, for

> What but the heart of youth can hold the story,
>> The young child's heart, so gentle and so wild,
> It can recall the magic of that Glory
>> That dreamed Itself into a little child.

Against the pangs of time are set the bravura of "The Mistletoe" and the hearty ode to "The Yule Yog," while the mystery of the incarnation is celebrated by "The Crib" and " 'They Found the Young Child' ". "The Crib" has something of the quality of a Blakean song of innocence, a beguiling simplicity which reveals cosmic overtones. A single five-line stanza tells the story:

> DAY closes in the cabin dim,
> They light the Christmas candle tall,
> For him who is the Light of all.
> They deck the little Crib for Him.
> Whose cradle is earth's swinging ball.

The thought is echoed in the final lines of "The Child

in the Manger," which conclude the volume:

> The Magi watched the heavens afar,
> Saw in the blue a starry stranger.
> But He whose playthings planets are
> Lay innocently in the manger.

"Susan Mitchell was more than a witty writer," AE said in his tribute; "she was a woman with a true spirituality which lit up the lyrics in her beautiful book of verse, *The Living Chalice*." He noted that many of the poems have "taken their place in the golden procession of Irish poetry," remaining in the memory because "some image of lovable and desirable life" illuminated them, and the image "flickered in the verse as a flame inside a lamp." In his appreciation of her poetry published in the next issue of *The Irish Statesman* two weeks later (March 27, 1926) AE chose four stanzas of "The Extravagant Heart" to "indicate the plenitude of her delight for the earth she lived on, in the friendships she had, in the life which never seemed to weary her." Yet Susan Mitchell, for all her love of life, was one for whom "this world was always casting up images of its Original." Such are the most fortunate:

> Those to whom life has these divine transparencies are happiest of all of us. These have perpetual compensations for what is perpetually passing away. Every moment heaps up some new beauty which is still the Ancient Beauty.

This is the mysticism of AE which became almost an orthodoxy with the poets of the Irish Revival. Yet AE generously points up the distance between his mystical earnestness and the almost unconscious responsiveness of his friend:

There are many people who have thought this without realising it. I think Susan Mitchell realised it hardly thinking about it at all. I am one of those who are always pondering over the mysteries, always imagining a delight in knowledge which but rarely comes to me.

Among the press opinions of the first edition were several which anticipated AE's final judgment. It was the time when the word "Celtic" carried its own magical aura; thus the Glasgow *Herald* found that "The true Celtic spirit—which is simply the pure essence of lyric poetry tinged with sadness and delicately misted with elusiveness—is present in Susan L. Mitchell's 'The Living Chalice.'" The *Times Literary Supplement* remarked on the union of "tenderness and beauty," and the *Freeman's Journal* of Dublin emphasized "the authentic sense of the deep mystery underlying the common things, and the intensity of emotion which makes life rich and expression moving." Miss Mitchell's unique combination of humor and pathos provided the reviewer in the *Irish Times* with one theme, the poet's simple sincerity:

> To rouse the laughter of men is one thing; to touch the tender cords of old memories, to awaken half-forgotten sadnesses, is another. The double gift is given to very few. . . . The absolute sincerity of feeling in these poems distinguishes them quite unmistakably from the mass of contemporary verse. . . . Here is no simulated rapture, wrought-up passion, or forced expression of feebly experienced griefs. . . . She did not sit down and write a lyric. The passionate regret was in her, and, to quote a phrase of her own, "it sang itself" into a poem.

4

George Moore (1916)

More causerie than criticism, Susan Mitchell's study of George Moore for the "Irishmen of Today" series affords a running commentary on aspects of the novelist's career, but turns aside for lively digressions. She remembers living with the Yeats family in London, where she read surreptitiously Moore's novel *The Mummer's Wife*, "chiefly, with feminine perversity, because W. B. Yeats had forbidden his sisters to read it." One hope was unfortunately not fulfilled: "what a lovely book I shall write some day about that most companionable household." She permits herself to comment on other titles in the series, and finds that "Mr. Darrell Figgis, who so ostentatiously presents us with a clue to the labyrinth of "AE," is lost in it himself." Joseph Hone, "one of the very few impartial Irish writers, is listless about Mr. Yeats, his book has no more blood in it than a balance sheet." In contrast, "There is blood" in St. John Ervine's account of Sir Edward Carson, the despised Ulster leader, though even here are qualifications: "he knows nothing about Sir Edward Carson, of course, but his teeth are firmly fixed in the calf of someone's leg, all the time, and he draws blood without a doubt." Surely an odd and paradoxical form of publicity for the venture!

The shock of the Easter 1916 Rising makes its impact on the closing pages of the book. As though it were impossible to concentrate on the task at hand in such tragic times, Miss Mitchell interrupts her concluding summary without warning:

> I write this last chapter of my book in a city that has been shattered by the big guns of modern warfare. It is a heavy ending for a book begun with a light heart. With every twenty-five years of Irish life we expect a tragedy, with every fifty years it inevitably comes. (p. 145)

Can England be so stupid, she asks, as to ignore the stubborn fact of Irish aspiration? The Irish cause "should appeal to a people like the English who were wont to love freedom themselves" and fought for it through centuries. Yet, in fairness to England, "She is surely in a desperate strait" at present, as evidenced by the suspension of liberties within her own borders, "a bad omen in a country which has grown great through its passion for individual liberty."

Like the often overlooked *Dublin Explorations & Reflections By An Englishman* (1917), these two pages carry the authentic note of urgent immediacy.

Also worthy of remark, before we get to the main topic, is the chapter describing the Dublin of the turn of the century:

Dublin at the time Mr. Moore came here was a very pleasant place to live in. It had all the ingredients of an agreeable literary society and a number of persons interested in art or literature or humanity either lived here or made the city frequent visits. George Moore said of Dublin that its "acoustic properties were perfect," so that no jest, be it whispered ever so softly in the closet, fails to be heard on the remotest house-top. It is an ideal home for clever talkers. (p. 89)

The last statement remains true today. Conversation spiced with gossip, enlivened by a sense of personality, and made pertinent by allusion, can still be enjoyed. Such an ambience is difficult to capture on the printed page. George Moore's *Hail and Farewell,* despite its presumptuousness, suggests something of this quality. The letters of John Butler Yeats, opinionated as they are, render well what Douglas Goldring, in *Dublin Explorations,* calls "The collection of 'knowledge,' or intellectual *bricabracologie,"* characteristic of the "provincial pedantry" of Dubliners. (p. 184) The essays of Moore's friend and disciple, Oliver St. John Gogarty, and, more recently, some of the effusions of Brendan Behan, are further instances.

Miss Mitchell characterizes the elder Yeats's art as having "the rare quality that he not only made his women pretty, any artist can do that, but he made them lovable, manifesting the interior beauty in their souls." Here it may not be out of place to quote Miss Mitchell's recollection of J.B.'s manner of painting a portrait. In her review of his *Essays Irish and American,* she described "The brave, tall figure, brush in hand, advancing on his canvas with great strides . . . putting on

touches with the ardour of one who would storm a
fortress, retreating as eagerly . . . talking enchantingly
all the time, his whole nature in movement." (*New Ireland,* November 2, 1918) Other artists included Walter
Osborne, "a charming companion and lovable man,"
and Jack Yeats, "whimsical and kindly, most winning
of all the Yeats." Moore's younger brother, Colonel
Maurice Moore, "might have attained a considerable
reputation as a writer" had he not turned to the
military organization of the National Volunteers. The
list continues: Hyde, Lady Gregory, Yeats, the pro-
fessors Mahaffy, Tyrrell, and Dowden, and, above all,
AE, who, though charged with being poet, painter, and
economist, "remains a friendly human being who loves a
laugh even at his own expense." The roll is impressive,
with Edward Martyn, Sir Horace Plunkett, Rolleston,
the two O'Grady scholars, Standish, "the noblest figure
of them all—a solitary, unconcerned with any movement, but himself an incarnation of the soul of Ireland,"
and his cousin, Standish Hayes O'Grady. The Fays of
the Abbey Theatre, the younger scholars Eglinton and
Best, and the second generation of poets—O'Sullivan,
Colum, Stephens, and the fledgling Oliver Gogarty,
"who had but just nipped the wires of the champagne
of his wit." So it goes on, culminating in one scarcely
known today, Commissioner Bailey, described as "clever,
discriminating, at whose hospitable house anything that
painted, sang, composed, or acted was sure of a welcome." In fact it was Bailey who held a farewell party
for George Moore on the eve of his return to London,
as we learn from the last pages of *Hail and Farewell.*

Among the guests, Moore writes, was "Susan Mitchell,
who sang songs about the friends I was leaving behind
me." Moore is also complimentary regarding Bailey,
speaking of his "alert and witty mind," remarking upon
his connoisseurship in books and pictures, "And, better
still, he practises life."

With this richness of talent to draw upon, Moore had
been fair to only a few of his acquaintances, Miss
Mitchell finds, among them John Eglinton, whose portrait is "genuine," and AE, who has been supplied "with
a halo he has no use for." He is "most flagrantly unjust"
in describing Douglas Hyde:

> How indignant one feels at the base caricature of one
> whose name in Ireland is beloved beyond most names
> . . . who by sheer force of personality created the move-
> ment in Ireland for the revival of Gaelic. . . . We who
> remember those days know what Ireland owes to Hyde's
> fiery spirit, his immense courage, his scholarship, his
> genius for organisation, his sincerity, his eloquence, and
> the kindness of his heart. (p. 83)

Moore's book is not autobiography, but "a work of
fiction improvised upon his friends and himself." Yet,
despite her resentment at *Hail and Farewell*, Miss
Mitchell remains unprejudiced in evaluating the novels.

His personality is another matter. His theatrical
absurdities are chronicled, from that letter to the *Irish
Times* on the grey mullet to his conversion to Protestantism. Throughout he is seen as "a society enter-
tainer," an actor playing before his mirror to an
audience of one. Most malicious is her account of his
painting. The entire chapter can easily be reproduced
here:

III

NOBODY in Ireland has ever seen any of Mr. Moore's paintings except "AE," to whom he once shyly showed a head, remarking that it had some "quality." "AE" remained silent. (p. 20)

Paradoxically his failure as a painter explains his success as an art critic. To him painting "was an unrequited love," and "We know as he writes about painting that his adoring eye is still on the palette which will never do his bidding." Moore once said of himself that "he loved the smell of oil paint better than the smell of flowers," and Miss Mitchell suspects that his rejection of Catholicism was attributable to the tastelessness of Irish churches.

Since his main theme as a novelist is love, Susan Mitchell begins by observing that in spite of a perverse literary theory, derived from the French, which sits uncomfortably upon him, "He has not created a wholly unpleasant woman, and some of his women are delightful beings, docile to life, mother-hearted, full of wonder and trust, illimitably kind," among them "Alice in 'Muslin,' Esther Waters, Kitty Hare, Agnes Lahens, Evelyn Innes." (p. 30) As for his frankness and vaunted knowledge of women, "Women know instinctively all he knows about love and more also." Had Moore been able to describe passion, we might be spared "his tiresome preoccupation with what one might call millinery and confectionery in the love adventures." He is too Irish to be, like a French novelist, "at home in his sins." "Perhaps the Latin races can sin gracefully, the Irish cannot," and though his creed is to be unashamed, "here I catch him tripping, for he is ashamed of being ashamed." (p. 34)

Esther Waters convinces one that it is written by a man with a heart, despite other evidence to the contrary, for in the central character we see "a woman refined, delicate, but in whom will and affection are so strong that her character begins to grow from the very moment when its destruction seemed inevitable." The author's preface to the 1899 edition "shows us a Moore whom perhaps many of his readers will not recognise and whose acquaintance, I imagine, Mr. Moore himself made with some surprise." She quotes his denial that the theme was the simple one of protesting the evil of gambling:

> "Betting may be an evil, but what is evil is always uncertain, whereas there can be no question that to refrain from judging others, from despising the poor in spirit and those who do not possess the wealth of the world is certain virtue. That all things that live are to be pitied is the lesson that I learn from reading my book, and that others may learn as much is my hope." (p. 46)

Unlike Dickens, "He does not look for the picturesque, but only traces the love of a mother for her child with a sincerity which, as I said before, was probably amazing to himself." The author's sympathy led Miss Mitchell almost to the point of saying, " 'For this thy sins be forgiven thee,' as the man in the audience at Fishamble Street theatre cried to the sinful woman who sang Handel's angel music at the first performance of the 'Messiah.' " A characteristically Dublin metaphor this, relying upon a local oral tradition dating from 1742.

In the memories and imaginations of Dubliners the streets still echo to the tread of eighteenth century figures.

The true George Moore, or perhaps it should be said, the best George Moore, is to be found in *Esther Waters, The Lake, The Untilled Field,* and parts of *Memoirs of My Dead Life,* "The Moore who is neither a mock satyr, nor a nasty little schoolboy, but a thinker and a warm-hearted human being." Of this Moore "we have fitful glimpses" even "in the waywardness of 'Ave, Salve and Vale.' "

Two chapters at the end of the book deal with Moore's recreation of the New Testament story in *The Brook Kerith.* Beginning with a mocking account of this modern Quixote travelling to the Holy Land in search of material, she turns surprisingly appreciative when evaluating the finished work. Calling it "a recital in a musical undertone," she happily describes its meditative charm by the metaphor of "a space of time filled with momentous happenings that yet fall silently as the sand in the hour-glass, and for all their meaning, there remains for us in the end but a little mound of sand." This tale of a Jesus of Nazareth recovered from an apparent rather than a real crucifixion aroused Susan Mitchell's fears that the Gospel story would be violated at the hands of a realist. Fortunately such was not the case, though questions may remain regarding Moore's similarity to "those rationalising writers who broke up the mould of the old pagan beliefs of Greece and Rome, making indeed a literature but defrauding the world of deity." In spite of being "an absorbing study in a rare psychology, as well as a complete realisation of a land of milk and honey," the work remains but "an epilogue to a beautiful story" written by one who "has no faith in any new vision, nothing wherewith to build up a new spiritual romance to make the world breathless with fresh beauty."

To Ireland Moore could have brought a quality of frankness that has been lacking in public life, while "his intense concern with human life and emotion might have imparted a warmth to our literature that is missing from it now." (p. 147) Had he not been hampered by his presuppositions about Ireland, handicapped by inappropriate literary theories, and, above all, "deflected by his own excessive egoism," his contribution to Irish culture might have been different. As it is:

> Mr. Yeats and his literary contemporaries in Ireland may have a more kindly, but they never will have a more brilliant chronicler. Literary history must accord Mr. Moore a place among the most brilliant and varied writers of our time. Still, he will be remembered less by the creations of his imagination than for his malicious and witty account of his contemporaries. (p. 149)

An interesting contemporary evaluation of the Mitchell study of George Moore is provided in the unsigned book by Douglas Goldring, *Dublin Explorations and Reflections by an Englishman,* mentioned above in regard to the conversational milieu. Because of Goldring's admiration for Moore's work he found her volume a disappointment, though he admitted to being "a little ashamed of himself for chuckling over it so gaily." It is too personal to do justice to the subject:

Her book is one of amusing personal anecdotes and is full
of the humourous and occasionally bitter chidings of an
attached friend. But throughout her study it is Mr. Moore
the man rather than Mr. Moore the writer with whom she
deals. Yet is it not in a man's lifework that the most
important part of him, the most enduring part, is to be
found? (p. 177)

Even in her admiration for *Esther Waters* "she scarcely
seems to conceal her fundamental lack of sympathy
with the writer's point of view."

Goldring continues to speak of depreciation, "and
depreciation of a particularly brilliant kind," as "one of
the characteristics of Dublin." He could be speaking
of George Moore as well as of Moore's mimic and
mocker; indeed, he finds the "seductive art" of depreciation common among writers, "but I have seldom seen
it brought to greater perfection than in Dublin":

One has the impression that if anyone in Dublin gets up
and does something, the other intellectuals stand round
and make destructive comments. And yet (so contradic-
tory is human nature) this love of depreciation exists co-
incidentally with a display of mutual admiration which
is positively disarming in its naïveté. (p. 179)

In *The Life of George Moore* (1936) Joseph Hone
reports that "Moore gave Miss Mitchell to understand
that she might write as freely about him as she liked,
take any liberties she would," but that he was offended
by the book:

The biographer had approached her subject in too face-
tious a spirit and seemed to regard Dublin's opinion as the
last word on Moore. But the injury that most rankled was
Miss Mitchell's neglect of all that he had said on the sub-

ject of the instinctive and far-off origins of his Protestantism. (pp. 330–331)

AE's defence of the Mitchell book aroused Moore's
suspicion "that A.E. had instigated many of the offending passages." Mr. Hone surmises that Moore's attitude
must have resembled that shown in his advice given to
Ernest Boyd, then engaged in writing *Ireland's Literary
Renaissance* (1916), the only comprehensive account
of the movement. Moore told Boyd that "I am part of
life like Yeats and Lady Gregory, and you have as
much right to sketch me as I had to sketch them, and
if your book have any value, its value will depend on
how much of yourself you put into it." Had he applied
this criterion to Susan Mitchell's study, he should have
had less occasion for resentment.

It may be expecting too much to hope that a vain
writer accept with graciousness a recounting of his personal foibles, but beyond this surface implication
George Moore might have detected an admiration for
his independence, in resisting "the temptation common
to every Irishman to obliterate himself in a movement."
He might also have come to respect Miss Mitchell's own
honesty of judgment, a candor which Robin Skelton
finds comparable to Moore's, but "more frequently
qualified by affection and dictated by principle." Mr.
Skelton emphasizes her courage in criticizing "those
articles of faith held so passionately by the leaders of
the Irish Renaissance." He cites her comment on the
emptiness of Irish political allegiances:

They value their municipal privileges more for the sense

of power these confer than from any serious intention of
using these powers for simple human needs and comforts.
Their political power has been treated as a game as divert-
ing as musical chairs at a children's party, sitting, acting
and voting to meaningless party tunes played at hazard
and stopped at hazard. (p. 142)

The result is portrayed as starkly by Miss Mitchell as
it might have been by Moore himself, or even Joyce.
She continues:

> If this were not so, would we have our land in grass, our
> towns and cities in slums, and our country without a
> human hope to break down the barriers that our several
> quests have imposed upon us? (pp. 142–143)

Among other insights, not mentioned by Mr. Skelton,
may be added her observation that few Irishmen dare
to be themselves:

> Is it any wonder that the inhabitants of a country such
> as ours, where so many creeds and parties clamour for a
> man's soul, cannot resist the temptation offered him of a
> comfortable pigeonhole retreat for it where it need never
> agitate him again?

Ireland is "A country where it is more convenient to
be anything rather than an Irishman" and where few
persons "walk about freely unclaimed by any Shib-
boleth." Moore is one of these rare beings:

> Ten years of Ireland couldn't fetter him. Neither the
> Gaelic League, the Nationalists, the Catholics or the
> Protestants could detain this slippery customer, and he
> left Ireland with a gibe for them all, sparing only those
> amongst his friends whose independence of mind and

indifference to his opinion perhaps protected them—"AE,"
John Eglinton, and Oliver Gogarty. (p. 63)

It is an interesting observation that all three of these
men subsequently left Ireland, as George Moore had,
and as James Joyce had done at the outset of his career.

Miss Mitchell is capable of acute insights into the
paralyzing blindness of religious bigotry, by no means
sparing her own Protestantism. She is skeptical even of
the effect upon Ireland of the literary revival itself:
"Has any intellectuality at all emerged out of it, any
public opinion, any essentially national flavour in our
life?" (p. 148) She senses the deadening growth of
mass culture—this in 1916!—in an Ireland "more and
more obsessed by the cinema and the penny novelette."
Such awareness suggests that her satiric verses are more
than clever jeux d'esprit; in fact they are the expressions
of an alert and critical intelligence.

5

The Laughter That Opens the Heart

Susan Mitchell's gaiety and charm remain in the memories of those who knew her, and its essence is preserved in her writing. Nevertheless, with occasional pieces such as hers, many would never be printed, or, if so, not collected. A diligent perusal of Dublin periodicals and fortunate finds in private libraries may uncover a number of others. A tentative list is included in an appendix.

Robin Skelton discovered an amusing playlet, "Leaguers and Peelers: or, The Apple Cart," in the October 1911 issue of *The Irish Review*. He has discussed this comic operetta in his essay on the writer in *The World of W. B. Yeats* (1965), and observes that though today it may appear "merely amusing," in its time "it must have seemed an outrage":

The parody of the National Anthem would have seemed

close to blasphemy, and Susan Mitchell did not avoid a similar accusation from Irish Nationalists, for her parodies of revered Irish songs are just as cruel, and her portrayal of the Irish is as comic as that of the British. (p. 236)

Though "cruel" may seem a bit too strong for this slight comedy, it is the parodies which give life and humor to the surprise-ending plot. Regrettably the point may be missed by those to whom the traditional airs are no longer familiar, as they once were in a vocally oriented society. Much of the humor is inevitably lost, as in all topical satire.

The situation centers upon an English prohibition of the use of Irish on signs. This ruling, which is still mentioned by older Dubliners, is attributed in an editorial note to "the dark ages," though the time is obviously present, that is, 1911. An apple-vendor is charged for having Gaelic lettering on his cart. The true wrong-doer is the judge's own daughter, a Gaelic League enthusiast:

> It was a Judge's daughter
> Who firmly took her stand
> Shoneens among, to learn the tongue
> That's dear to Ireland.

Inasmuch as she is a minor, the judge himself is guilty. He laments:

Johanna has joined the Gaelic League, a thing I can't abide,
And for her crime I must commit judicial suicide.

Only the hero's sacrifice redeems the situation, as he

volunteers to serve the sentence, and thereby win Johanna.

The skit opens with a chorus of constables, whose chants are based on "The British Grenadiers," "Rule Britannia," and "God Save the King":

> There's treason in the pale,
> A rising of the Gael;
>   Oh hear me call!
> Help, or we'll lose our pay;
> And our majestic sway,
> Roast beef from day to day,
>   Lord, save us all!

The national anthem is also sung by the foreman of the jury, whose aria ends:

> Who speaks a foreign tongue
> Good Irishmen among
> Oh, let his neck be wrung.
> God save the King.

The foreman is dazzled by the outcome, as still another feat of justice:

> We who oft watched with reverence and awe
> The glorious miracle of British law
> And felt how it inevitably must
> Surprise alike the just and the unjust.

In 1918 there appeared a delightful book of Dublin verse which deserves to be rescued from oblivion. The appropriately entitled *Secret Springs of Dublin Song* reveals an Ireland in motley, recording the wit and persiflage which accompanied the more serious literary efforts of the time. "The verses reel at times, are heady or frothy, and one catches a whiff of the spirituous atmosphere of the town," Miss Mitchell wrote in her preface. The thirty-three poems are unsigned, but their authorship was something of an open secret. Miss Mitchell, in fact, claimed to be "more confident of obscurity" while "disguised in my own name," than the anonymous contributors. These are, she continued, "Idle fancies, whimsical fancies, conscienceless objectors to the legitimate service of literature." Oliver St. John Gogarty and Seumas O'Sullivan were responsible for most of the contents, however irresponsible they be. Never wholly irresponsible, though, for when Gogarty salutes the shameless hussy Spring he also observes that "Dublin sends by dirt and rheum/ Brigades of babies to the tomb." For his part O'Sullivan can contribute the dramatic monologue of the slum child ("Ambition in Cuffe Street") which opens:

> When I grow big I'll smoke and swear
> And drink like my old fellow there. . . .

There is self mockery too, as in O'Sullivan's satire of the Celtic Twilight, beginning "Child, there are mists in my mind." Tyrrell's parodies are preserved, the macabre ballad "Johnny, I Hardly Knew You" rendered in Dublinese, Swinburnese, and Miltonese. But this takes us away from Susan Mitchell, whose role in the collection seems minor indeed.

Another work of interest remains to be mentioned. The County Armagh Museum has a manuscript notebook of her poems, with illustrations by AE. The volume, noted by Alan Denson in his bibliography of AE, opens with a four-line invocation of Celtic vision:

A darkness heavier than night hung over Sligo Bay
  What a dawn awoke in me
When I saw a ship of flame come sailing under Knocknarea
  Up the river from the sea!

At the foot of the page AE has sketched a darkened landscape, with cottages along the water's edge, and a square-sailed ship ablaze with flame in the midst of the river. There are about fifteen of these mystical drawings, mostly of angelic figures. The drawings are concentrated within the first half of the 94 page notebook. Thirteen of the thirty poems in the manuscript have not been collected. It is unnecessary to deal with many of them, as they echo the poet's usual themes. An exception must be made for the tiny fragment, "A Star," in which the short lines suggest the delicacy of James Stephens:

> A star
> Tender and faint
> Love shone afar
> To my eyes came
> Piercing and white
> His flame
> Nigher
> Nigher and nigher
> Crept to my heart
> His fire
> A star
> He bore me up
> To shine afar.

The poignancy in "The Way of Grief" may be illustrated by the conclusion of the first stanza:

I know at last this is indeed my way
This darkness is the dawning of my day.

The tragic beauty of spiritual vision is also evoked in
these lines from an untitled poem:

> I asked but for the opened eye
> To see Thy Glory passing by
> Nor dreamed the woe the being knows
> When all its myriad eyes unclose.

The single stanza concludes with a state of metaphysical
shock: "Amazed and shelterless I go." A similar quality
is attained in an eight-line invocation to St. Patrick,
from whose presence the demons were miraculously dis-
pelled. The poem ends, prayerfully:

> We are Patrick's children, to high hopes we cling
> Give us Patrick's courage and his comforting.

This poem is dated "Jan. 1920" and thus has special
relevance to the "Time of the Troubles" which Ireland
was suffering at the hands of undisciplined English sol-
diers, the 'Black and Tans.'

Lighter verse is also included, most of it unfinished.
Bits on the Museum restaurant, on the food tax of 1903,
on the Dublin visit of Victoria are not up to her best.
"The Rime of the Little Curate" is better, conveying
in its smirking tones the prissy sanctimoniousness of
such a character, who might have come straight from
the pages of Jane Austen. The first stanza reads:

> I'm but a little curate
> And small my salary
> And yet there's many a Rector
> Might envy little me

> I'm such a very happy
> And busy little bee.

The rector is an image of contented complacency:

> I'll never drive a carriage
> I'll never wed a wife
> For thoughts of love & marriage
> May lead to woe & strife
> And busy little curates
> Must lead a peaceful life.

It seems appropriate to conclude in this light vein, with the little rector, whoever he might have been, missing immortality and disappearing from our sight amid a cascade of hearty Irish laughter. Among her last book notices, published less than four months before her death, were short reviews of two Irish humorists, Percy French and M. J. MacManus. Her comments show an awareness that the new, emerging Ireland was losing some of the lightheartedness the nation once had: "We have deteriorated in good nature as well as in wit," she wrote in regard to French's "boyish innocence and love of fun." (November 14, 1925) Yet Irish humor never seems to die, for MacManus "is shaping for a very good parodist" in *A Green Jackdaw* (November 28, 1925). Her words of praise for this new talent may well apply to her own work:

> I hope Mr. MacManus will go on writing verse to make us laugh at ourselves, for no laughter so opens the heart.

Selected Bibliography

AE (George William Russell), ed. *A Celtic Christmas*, annual holiday supplement of *The Irish Homestead*. Susan Mitchell contributed:

1902 (unsigned) "The Army of the Voice," p. 25.
1903 (S. L. M.) "Homeless," p. 7.
    (S. L. M.) "The Living Chalice," p. 21.
    (unsigned skit) "The Voice of One," p. 22.
1904 (Susan L. Mitchell) "The Greenlands," p. 17.
    (unsigned stanza on Moore) "Moods and Memories," beginning "If you like a stir," in a section of parodies headed "The Celtic Renaissance Birthday Book." Susan Mitchell herself is parodied by a quatrain, "The Muse in the Wardrobe," p. 15.
1905 (Susan L. Mitchell) "Ireland," p. 19, with illustration by AE.
    Four unsigned satires, under title, "Ballads of the Year 1905," the first two later in *Aids*, the third in "Leaguers and Peelers," *The Irish Review* (1911), the fourth uncollected: "The High Sheriff for Mayo," "The Ballad of Shawe Taylor," "Who Fears to Write His Gaelic Name?" and "The Nightmayor." The editor regrets his inability to print other verses, including "Our minstrel Hyde to the States has gone," of which

he quotes the last quatrain. He also refers to "The Lost Tune" and to "a fiery version . . . of a speech made at a Dublin Corporation meeting." pp. 8–9.

1906 (S. L. M.) "A Dream," p. 5, with illustration by AE.

1907 (Susan L. Mitchell) "Immortality," p. 10.

1908 (Susan L. Mitchell) "Christmas" (later "The Mistletoe"), p. 9.

AE, ed. *New Songs . . . by Padriac Colum, Eva Gore-Booth, Thomas Keohler, Alice Milligan, Susan Mitchell, Seumas O'Sullivan, George Roberts, and Ella Young.* Dublin: O'Donoghue & Co.; London: A. H. Bullen, 1904. Mauve boards, white paper label. 58 pp. Frontispiece woodcut, "The Plougher," by Jack B. Yeats. Three editions were issued in 1904. See Alan Denson, *Printed Writings by George W. Russell: A Bibliography* (Evanston: Northwestern University Press, 1961), items 70, 70 A, and 70 B for description. Miss Mitchell's poems are:

"Love's Mendicant" (p. 20)

"The Living Chalice" (p. 25) Earlier in *A Celtic Christmas,* 1903

"The Lonely" (later entitled "Loneliness") (p. 29)

"Amergin" (p. 33)

"The Army of the Voice" (p. 54) Earlier in *A Celtic Christmas,* 1902

The Abbey Row, Not Edited by W. B. Yeats. Dublin: Maunsel. n.d. [1907] Green paper wrappers, with woodcut on cover. 12 pp. Susan Mitchell contributed "Oh, No! We Never Mention It!" pp. 10, 12, signed "S," and possibly some of the other verse.

Aids to the Immortality of Certain Persons in Ireland, Charitably Administered by Susan L. Mitchell. Dublin: New Nation Press, 1908. Brown paper wrappers, with panel on cover by Beatrice Elvery, depicting, standing in a line, Edward Martyn, W. B. Yeats, George Moore, Anthony MacDonnell, Douglas Hyde, AE, Horace Plunkett, Hugh

Lane, William Orpen, and Captain John Shawe-Taylor. 40 pp. See Seumas O'Sullivan, *Essays and Recollections,* Dublin: Talbot Press, 1944, p. 124.

The Living Chalice and Other Poems, by Susan L. Mitchell, Being Number Six of the Tower Press Booklets, Second Series. Dublin: Maunsel, 1908. Blue paper, with woodcut of ruined round tower on cover. 36 pp. Adds nineteen poems to the five from *New Songs,* making twenty-four.

Cooke, John, ed. *The Dublin Book of Irish Verse.* Dublin: Hodges, Figgis; and London: Henry Frowde, Oxford University Press, 1909. Includes:
"Immortality" (#475)
"Amergin" (#476)
"Homeless" (#477)
"Exile" (#478)

"Leaguers and Peelers; or, the Apple Cart," *The Irish Review,* I, #9 (October 1911) 390–406.

Frankincense and Myrrh. Dublin: Cuala Press, 1912. Rosette design on cover, frontispiece in color depicting adoration of the magi. 16 pp. Eleven poems, four of them reprinted from *The Living Chalice,* 1908.

The Living Chalice and Other Poems. Dublin and London: Maunsel, 1913. Blue cloth, vellum backstrip. 56 pp. To the twenty-four poems in the 1908 edition are added six from *Frankincense and Myrrh* ("The Star in the East" is not reprinted) and thirteen new poems, making a total of forty-three.

Aids to the Immortality of Certain Persons in Ireland, Charitably Administered by Susan L. Mitchell. Dublin and London: Maunsel, 1913. Blue cloth, vellum backstrip. 89 pp. An enlarged edition.

Graves, Alfred P., ed. *The Book of Irish Poetry.* London: T. Fisher Unwin, n.d. [1914] Includes: "Carrick" (pp. 297–298)

George Moore, by Susan L. Mitchell. "Irishmen of To-Day" series. Dublin and London: Maunsel & Co., 1916. Blue cloth. 149 pp.

Secret Springs of Dublin Song. Dublin: The Talbot Press; London: T. Fisher Unwin, 1918. Brown cloth. Edition limited to 500 numbered copies. xii and 51 pp. Miss Mitchell contributed the signed "Preface" and, according to a copy signed by Oliver Gogarty (Bucknell University Library), she was responsible for the first poem, "Epigram to the Authors," initialed "M. S.", though the poem has been attributed to "Michael Scot" (Miss Kathleen Goodfellow), as in the copy described in Alan Denson's bibliography of A.E. (see above under *New Songs*) and in the Sligo County Library copy, as reported by Miss Nora Niland.

Robinson, Lennox, ed. *A Golden Treasury of Irish Verse.* London: Macmillan, 1925. Includes:
"The Descent of the Child" (# ccxix)
"Immortality" (# ccxxxi)

Christmas Poems. Privately printed, Christmas 1934. With introductory poem, "In Memory of Susan Mitchell" by M. J. Mac M[anus]. 10 pp.

Hoagland, Kathleen, ed. *1000 Years of Irish Poetry.* New York: Devin-Adair, 1947. Includes:
"The Irish Council Bill, 1907" (p. 299)
"Ambition in Cuffe Street" (p. 710) Surely wrongly attributed. This poem, from *Secret Springs . . .* is always given to Seumas O'Sullivan, as it is in the Cuala Press *Broadside* of October 1909.

Garrity, Devin A., ed. *The Mentor Book of Irish Poetry.* New York: New American Library, 1965. Includes "The Wind Bloweth Where It Listeth" (p. 281)

SOME UNCOLLECTED POEMS

Titles are in parentheses. "A" indicates Armagh Co.

Museum MS, paginated by compiler; "C" Cuala Press Christmas cards, with serial number; "L", *The Lady of the House,* Christmas numbers; "S", *Studies,* VII (Sept. 1918), p. 445. The "L" and "S" poems have not been seen, but are derived from Alan Denson's note in his edition of AE's letters, and supplied by the kindness of Patrick Henchy, Director, National Library of Ireland.

(*Christmas Tree, The*)	L 1915
"Come gather round me, neighbors"	Kain postcard
"A darkness heavier than night hung over Sligo Bay"	A 1
"The day burns to its close" (*A Nursery Song for Christmas Eve*)	C 126
"Dear hand that held me" (*The Way of Grief*)	A 41
"Do you hear the schoolboys crying" (*The Bleat of the Children*) Ir. Statesman, December	6, 1924
(*Dublin Tenements, The*)	L 1913
"Father and mother pace the shore" (*Sligo Bay*)	S
"From funeral unto funeral thou" (*To a Tall Silk Hat*) Madras, India *Mail,* 16 Sept. 1924, from *Irish Statesman* (no date given)	
"His coming set the world aflame" (*The Star in the East*)	C 14
"Home Rule is still far off" (add'l stanza to The Irish Council Bill; see Robin Skelton, *The Irish Book,* I, 4 (1962), 104)	
"I asked but for the opened eye"	A 63
"I'm but a little curate" (*The Rime of the Little Curate*)	A 89
"In Dublin's old museum (*Departmental Ditties*)	A 75
(*Irish Bombadier, The*)	L 1922
"It was from Dublin Castle"	Curran MS
"I've walked about the world with its wide sands"	A 51
"I will arise and go now, and go to Grafton Street"	Kain MS

"John Bull was a very dull old boy" (*Fiscality*
A Ballad of October 1903)   A 81
"My wild will spreads its wings and flies"   A 31
"No mistake this time" (*Irish Convention Num-*
ber Two. A.D. 1920)   L 1918
"On a hill in Erin flapping sombre wing"   A 69
"One set the doorway of my house ajar" (*The*
Arrows of Light)   A 65
"Our pretty Beatrice departs" Cf. Lady Glenavy,
"Today We Will Only Gossip" (1964), p. 69
" 'A pity,' says Victoria" (*Dublin Visit of Victoria*) A 85
(*Sorrowful Birth, The*)   L 1915
"Stay thee awhile, upspringing heart" (*Christmas*) C 60
"A star"   A 33
"There are troublesome nations still existing"
(*Troublesome Nations*)   L 1920
"To dance or not to dance, that is
the question"   *Ir. Statesman*, Aug. 30, 1924
"To these high lands a stranger" Also in
Frankincense ... (1912)   C 69
(*The Wail of the Pseudo-Gael*)   L 1923
"We who know Time's little ways"   C 122
"What of the worldless [*sic*] voices of the Earth" A 53

ADDITIONAL NOTE

Mr. Alan Denson's exhaustive work, *James H. Cousins and Margaret E. Cousins: A Bio-Bibliographical Survey* (Kendal, Alan Denson, 1967) calls attention to a number of Susan Mitchell items, and his correspondence with me has added still more. Miss Mitchell's work was noted by Mary C. Sturgeon *Studies of Contemporary Poets* (London: George G. Harrap, 1916) and by Cousins in the second edition (1919) of his *New Ways in English Literature*, first published three years before. In the added chapter on "Some Poets of the Irish Renaissance" (pp. 86–94) he speaks of her sense of "a spiritual realm, a kingdom of certainty and repose behind the fluctuant details of this realm of life that obscures the inner and true world. Hence Miss Mitchell sings of immortality."

Mr. Denson also observes the reference by Maire Nic Shiubhlaigh (*Ang.* Marie Walker), *The Splendid Years* (1955) to a proposed "bi-lingual pantomime" of 1908 or 1909, with "a distinct political flavour," to be written by AE and Susan Mitchell, with others. The political emphasis would be in keeping with the Theatre of Ireland group, which had seceded from the Abbey Theatre in order to emphasize political activism. (Denson, pp. 234, 42, 344; Nic Shiubhlaigh, p. 142).

In a recent letter Mr. Denson mentions a brochure, *Carrick-on-Shannon,* which describes the town and cites Susan Mitchell as a celebrated native.